I0148893

What people are saying about…

This is a book that will help Christians follow hard after Christ, help husbands and wives love their spouses, and call ordinary men and women towards the extraordinary task of being faithful in the little things. If you're looking to put the most important things first in your life, this book will be a great help to you.

- Drew Byers

Associate Pastor – First Baptist Church

Athens, TN

T.K. does an extraordinary job at asking the question every Christian ought to be asking daily. This book takes you on the writer's own personal journey, one that is deeply relatable. It reminds us that in every station of life, our sinful hearts are subject to lead us chasing towards vanity. So, whether it is the pastor chasing ministerial "success" or a member searching for happiness, TK's words provoke a deep self-reflection, that if honest, should be followed by repentance.

- Jeremy Berry

Lead Pastor – New Heights Church

Hurricane, WV

WHAT ARE WE CHASING?

T.K. KING

FOREWORD BY WILL BASHAM

WHAT ARE WE
CHASING?

BECOMING
BETTER CHASERS
OF EVERYTHING IN LIFE

REFOCUSING OUR VISION ON
GOD AND FAMILY

TORNADO HOUSE PUBLISHING

What Are We Chasing?

Published by Tornado House Publishing

Copyright © 2018 T.K. King

All Rights Reserved

Cover Design by

Dustin Harper | dustinharperwv@gmail.com

Aubrey Meadows | bybredesigns@gmail.com

Back Cover Photography by

Hannah Kelly | wearethekellys.com

All rights reserved. No part of this publication may be produced, stored in a retrieval system, or transmitted in any form or by any means – electronic, mechanical, photocopy, recording or otherwise – without the prior permission of the author. The Holy Bible, English Standard Version® (ESV®). Copyright © 2001 by Crossway, a publishing ministry of Good News Publishers. All rights reserved. ESV Text Edition: 2016. Bolding of scripture has been added by the author for emphasis. The Holy Bible, English Standard Version (ESV) is adapted from the Revised Standard Version of the Bible, copyright Division of Christian Education of the National Council of the Churches of Christ in the U.S.A. All rights reserved.

Paperback ISBN: 978-0692139936

To my beautiful, strong, encouraging wife, Charity:

Thank you. Thank you for loving me when I acted as though I loved other things more than you. Thank you for never giving up and always being supportive of me pursuing my dreams. You are my rock and my love.

Other Acknowledgments:

To my New Heights pastors: My job, my career, my walk with God, and especially my marriage would never be where it is today without you guys. You are always loving and bluntly truthful. I'm sure you never thought I would say it, but I am incredibly thankful that God brought Charity and I to West Virginia.

To my New Heights family: You guys rock! I've never felt so welcomed into a body of believers and treated with such respect and friendship as I have at NH. It is a joy and an honor to serve Jesus with every single one of you. Glorify! Grow! Go!

To my parents and grandparents: I could never have made it to where I am today without the incredible guidance of you all, and I couldn't ask for or imagine a better family. I love you with all my heart, and I pray that Charity and I can be as wonderful of parents and grandparents as you have been to us.

Other Acknowledgments:

To those who helped complete and edit this book:
This book would be nowhere near its current state if it wasn't for your ideas, thoughts, feedback, critiques, countless phone calls, meetings, and desire to see this book be as good as it could be.

Charity King, Will Basham, Jeremy Berry, Drew Byers, and the many others who encouraged me along the way. Your effort and input are highly honored, and I am blessed to know and work with each of you. Thank you.

Contents

foreword

As a dad of five young children, I spend a lot of time chasing. Chasing my kids down teaches me a lot about how our Heavenly Father relentlessly pursues us. I chase them for different reasons: sometimes to punish them, sometimes to hug them, sometimes to save them. Regardless of the reasons, there are always valuable lessons in the chase.

Our God models the chase for us. He pursues His own glory and pursues us toward that end. He shows us what is proper for us to chase after, if we would only listen. Our rebel hearts lead us into our own pursuits while we are pursued not only by God, but also by the enemy. Proverbs 13:21 says, "Disaster pursues sinners, but the righteous are rewarded with good."

In "What Are We Chasing?", TK does a phenomenal job at reorienting (or orienting) our hearts toward proper priorities. Our affections, desires, passions, and pursuits make up our "chase," as we run the race of life. Just a small deviation from God's will, over time, will lead us far from the goal. TK writes from his own soul as he presents a bold and honest work of transparency. TK's example of redirection is a breath of fresh air for any believer.

So jump in and do an honest assessment of your life. What are you chasing? Steer your heart toward God's will instead of your own. As TK will explore, the benefits are abundant, and the glory of God is worth it. "Whoever pursues righteousness and kindness will find life, righteousness, and honor." - Proverbs 21:21

- Will Basham

Planting Pastor of New Heights Church

Milton, WV

introduction

One of the worst things about being a worship leader or a pastor is that you very seldom just get to go to church and be fed by other leaders or pastors. Instead, you're always feeding, and that can be extremely taxing. Thankfully, my pastors see that need to be fed and really encourage the worship leaders at my church to take Sundays off, rest, and attend worship conferences where we can be fed by some of the best worship leaders out there. And that, dear reader, is where this story begins.

In May of 2017 four of us from the worship team at our church set out to attend LIFT conference at Passion City Church in Atlanta, GA. If you aren't familiar with LIFT, it's a gathering of worship leaders and worship teams to focus their minds and hearts back around God and to hear from other great worship leaders and teams about how they execute worship in their congregations. There are main sessions with music and a speaker and then breakout sessions that you can pick based on what topics and principles you see as beneficial to your church and worship team. It's really awesome! This was my first time attending, and I would recommend it to anyone!

Although the tail end of this trip didn't end well for me (mostly because I got a stomach virus and spent the second day of the conference laying out in the car feeling sick) the beginning of the conference sparked everything that would lead me and my wife to a happier marriage, my job/career to a more enjoyable work flow, and to me writing this book.

Walking into the conference felt amazing! Everything was set up just like I imagined it should be. There were plenty of volunteers, and they all made us feel extremely welcome. The worship setting felt warm and inviting, and you could tell everything was very well planned. It was a perfect environment for God to move. However, I never expected Him to move in the way that He did.

If you are a worship leader, musician, or even a pastor, you understand the struggle of attending conferences or events where there are other people playing and preaching. It's almost impossible not to sit there and critique the whole time, right?! And as the Passion band took the stage and started the conference, that's what I began to do.

I'm not even sure I was aware of it then, but looking back now, critiquing is exactly what I was doing. I was watching how the worship leaders were acting on stage

Even in the midst of all my judging, critiquing, and skewed focus during worship, God still moved!

and seeing how they transitioned in between the songs. I was critiquing the mix and thinking about how I would adjust levels, EQ, and compression if I was running sound. But, what's weird and absolutely amazing, is that even in the midst of all my judging, critiquing, and skewed focus during worship, God still moved!

God knew I needed a change in my life, and He had chosen that exact moment to reveal it to me. And, there's nothing I could have been doing or thinking that would have stopped Him.

Let me back up. Even though I was critiquing everything about the worship experience, I was still worshiping. It was a sad, effortless worship, but I was singing and really trying to worship. And, as I stood there singing and yes, judging, I was hit with the question, "What am I chasing?" It wasn't an audible voice, and I have no recollection as to what I was thinking or singing when I thought that. But, that question just randomly popped into my head.

As I sat there pondering that question, I realized how jacked up my life had become. I had been chasing the wrong things with the wrong purpose, and it was literally tearing me and my marriage a part. I knew as soon as I came back home, I had to make some changes. Thankfully, that wasn't just a "moment" I had; I actually came back and made some changes! And wow! I've seen

God move in more ways than I could ever imagine, and He hasn't stopped!

I feel like in a typical situation, someone would have that experience, come home, make the changes, see the drastic differences over the course of a few years, and then sit down to write about it. That's not at all how I approached writing this book. I started writing this book merely a few days after coming back from that conference with only the untried principles that were bursting from my soul! And I knew, if I didn't talk about it, write about it, and really flesh it out, I wouldn't be able to do it.

So, this book is more than just a documentation of my journey; it is my journey. And as you read and begin yours, know that I'm right there struggling with you, making mistakes, and still not having it figured out. None of us are perfect and we never will be perfect until we are made complete in Jesus. I'm still learning and just getting started on the incredible journey God has for my life, my marriage, and my family.

This book will be tough, and I'll ask you to do things you aren't comfortable with. That's okay! It's going to be uncomfortable for me too. But, be encouraged! I know that we can make it, and I know God has incredible things in store for us. Becoming a better chaser won't be easy, and it will take time. Be patient with yourself and your progress. I promise you'll see results and feel less burdened in your life and closer to God and those around you. Take a deep breath. Let's look at what we are chasing and what we should be chasing. We'll make some adjustments and become better chasers together!

chapter one

CHASING

In order to properly figure out what we are chasing and discover how to chase something well, we need to understand what it means to chase. My favorite definition that I have found goes like this: "to follow or devote one's attention to with the hope of attracting, winning, gaining, etc." [1] In this definition, there is an action (follow or devote your attention) and there is a purpose (attracting, winning, or gaining).

Take a few minutes and think about what you follow or devote your attention to. That could be anything from a sporting team you are on, a lady's luncheon you speak at every week, working out, or a new boyfriend/girlfriend. Basically, where do you spend your time and energy? Then, ask yourself why and what is the purpose of each particular chase. Turn to the Chasing Workbook on page 167 and jot these down now, or feel free to grab a notebook. They will be essential to working your way through this book and learning how to become a better chaser. If you don't want to write in the book, the workbook is available at www.whatarewechasing.com.

As I write this book, I am learning and being encouraged as well and am constantly trying to be a better chaser. Below I will list a few things that I was chasing, why I was chasing them, and tell you a little bit about myself. Hopefully, you can see where I am coming from and how I have implemented the principles outlined in this book as we go through each chapter.

1. CAREER

This was the number one thing I was chasing when I was hit with the question, "What am I chasing?" I work as a Creative Arts Director for New Heights Church in WV, co-own a record label and music company, and own and run a recording studio out of my home. Seventy-five percent of my work for the church and label/studio is done from inside my home studio. This, in itself, has posed a significant problem in being intentional about what I chase, but we will get to that in a later chapter.

The reason I was chasing my career was to provide a better future for my family and currently support them. Sounds good right? While providing a better future for my family and making money to pay the bills is a great thing, it's not the most important thing and should never be what I spend the majority of my time and energy chasing. Chasing your career, job, or

> Chasing your career, job, or finances is a quick way to come face to face with exhaustion and frustration.

finances is a quick way to come face to face with exhaustion and frustration if you make it priority number one. It can also be so unrewarding and unfulfilling, which you will shortly discover is very important. Let's look at a few verses from Proverbs 10.

> *"Treasures gained by wickedness do not profit, but righteousness delivers from death...The wage of the righteous leads to life, the gain of the wicked to sin...The blessing of the Lord makes rich, and he adds no sorrow with it...Doing wrong is like a joke to a fool, but wisdom is pleasure to a man of understanding...The hope of the righteous brings joy, but the expectation of the wicked will perish..."* [2]

God's desire is for us to be fulfilled by chasing Him, not all the other things we chase. While much of the exhaustion and frustration we experience from our failed chases is mostly bad, there can be healthy exhaustion and frustration. As you'll soon discover, if you haven't already, chasing after God can lead to those things, even chasing after Him properly. But even through that exhaustion and frustration, God will bless, and you will experience that reward and renewing of your spirit.

2. FAMILY

I've always known that family was important and before getting married, I promised myself I would chase my wife, lead her well, and pray and read scripture with her daily. While the latter part sounds easy and, honestly, takes 10-15 minutes every day, I found it to be one of the most difficult things I've ever had to do, and I still struggle with it. Though setting aside the time to do it is important, it's not only

> You can lead a frustrated family, but you can't lead a family frustrated.

about the time; it's about the heart. If you are chasing other things that are causing you to be exhausted and frustrated, your heart (desire) is not going to want to spend that little extra time leading your wife or family. You can lead a frustrated family (and I promise, if you haven't seen it yet, you will), but you can't lead a family frustrated. And because I was chasing my career, I was constantly frustrated and failed to chase my family well.

3. GOD

I was saved when I was nine and have always, to different degrees, been pursuing my relationship with God. Growing up in church and having a good Christian family made it very easy to be surrounded by God and the things Christians were "supposed to do" (read the Bible, pray, etc.). But, that made it very easy to focus on others and never truly get involved and focus on MY relationship with God. And, I've found that working for a church creates the same scenario. It's incredibly easy to fall into the rut of being content with your relationship with God and not seeking to know Him more or become more like Jesus. While having a good relationship with God and being happy with your walk is great, we should never be content with it, and it's taken me this long to realize that.

There's a big difference between being

There's a big difference between being content with your relationship with God and being satisfied with it.

content with your relationship with God and being satisfied with it. I love my walk with God and it truly makes me happy, but I should never get content and stop pursuing Him. We should always desire to know God more, learn more about Him, and become more like Jesus. Unless we are wholeheartedly chasing after God, that can be a very difficult task.

Now, onto why I was chasing God. I feel like I've always desired to chase God for the right reasons, but

He never made it to the top of my chasing list. It always seemed to be one of those things that I said I would get around to and never did. That's why being intentional and purposeful about your chases is so important. If you don't direct your heart and develop a clear focus and vision of what you are chasing, you might as well be chasing the sun and running off into the distance as the credits begin to roll.

4. FACEBOOK

Yes. It's possible. I was chasing Facebook. Every free moment: Facebook. During an ad on Netflix: Facebook. Waiting in line: Facebook. Toilet: Facebook. Every free moment I had where my brain was not focused on something, I reverted to…Facebook.

Why are we so attracted (well…more like addicted) to Facebook?! Is it the constant status updates from our friends or celebrities we love? Or maybe it's the joyous feeling of having a new message, only to find it's a message from Facebook letting you know you've gained a new "friend". Or maybe, it's the calming massaging our thumbs experience while swiping up and down. Whatever it is, my soul craved it. Deleting the Facebook app on my phone was the first step I took in becoming a better chaser. We will look more into that in chapter two.

If you're like me, it can be a rude awakening when you honestly consider what you are chasing and the reasons behind it. As I sat there at LIFT conference (see introduction) and asked myself the question, "What am I chasing?", I was ashamed to be truthful and accept the fact that I wasn't chasing the right things, or at least not with the proper focus and energy. I had spent the last two years of my marriage convincing myself that what I was chasing was important, but I never felt like I was getting anywhere. I always felt tired and that my efforts weren't enough to build a Godly relationship, lead my family well, or create a career that I was happy with and one that supported my family. And when I realized why I continuously felt this way and took the proper steps to fix it, it was almost an immediate change. I am so excited to be on this journey with you to a lifestyle of rewarding and purposeful chasing!

CHASING MAKES YOU TIRED

Have you ever played a game that involved chasing, such as tag, or had a sibling that did something so atrocious you had to chase them down and let 'em have it? Though both of these things can be fun, there's no doubt that they make you tired. You run and run and run until hopefully you catch them, and then you spend the next few minutes breathing heavily and gaining your energy back.

Chasing things in life yield the same results. The more and longer you chase something, the more exhausted you get. And in both instances, since you are only one person who can only be in one place, you can, for the most part, only chase one thing at a time. There are some occasions where you can chase multiple things at a time, but the primary goal is to find a healthy balance of switching between what you are chasing and giving them their proper time and effort based on their priority.

Now, back to the game of tag or chasing your sibling. Without the reward of catching them, you will become even more exhausted and frustrated. Theoretically, whether or not you catch them is not going to determine how tired you are. I mean, if not catching them requires more running, then yes. Obviously, that would make you tired. But the sheer fact that if you run the same distance with the same effort, whether or not you catch them will not physically have an effect on the amount of lactic acid in your muscles. It's a mind game. When you catch them, you get excited and filled with adrenaline in such a way that you may not notice how tired and worn out your muscles have become. That's the beauty of the reward. When we constantly chase after God and are focused on that reward, or prize, as Paul puts it, we won't notice the other things in life that typically wear us down when we aren't focused on Jesus.

"Not that I have already obtained this or am already perfect, but I press on to make it my own, because Christ Jesus has made me his own. Brothers, I do not consider that I have made it my own. But one thing I do: forgetting what lies behind and straining forward to what lies ahead,

I press on toward the goal for the prize of the upward call of God in Christ Jesus."

- Philippians 3:12-14

The problem I've faced over the last several years is that I've been chasing things that I rarely, if ever, "gain" on or "win" at and seldom see a reward. The result? Exhaustion and frustration. In order to be successful chasers, we have to chase things that are rewarding and renew our spirit to keep chasing.

THE REWARD

Who doesn't like a good reward? It makes us feel good about ourselves and

In order to be successful chasers, we have to chase things that are rewarding and renew our spirit to keep chasing.

affirms that we have accomplished something. Likewise, when we work towards something and expect to get a reward for doing so and then don't, it can cause a lot of problems in our life. Depending on the significance of what we were expecting the reward to be, it can lead us to exhaustion, frustration, anger, jealousy, depression, or even worse.

Have you ever heard the saying "the cake is a lie"? Basically, it means that the reward that you were expecting was a lie and you didn't get anything. I've used the saying for years and never considered its deep implications to the principles in this book until I started writing this paragraph. Whether or not you've heard or used that saying, let's just agree that it sucks to not be rewarded when you've worked hard for something and you were expecting a reward.

A rather recent instance of this really got to me, and you'll see why. The record label that I co-own makes a lot of purchases around the $300-500 range, including anything from CDs or other merchandise for our artists to studio rentals. There was a charge for around $400 that somehow got listed under the wrong account and ended up being a fraud charge. Once we discovered this charge, we contacted our bank and they, reluctantly, said they would fix it. I'm guessing their hesitation was that it wasn't a super recent charge. Either way, they said they would fix it. Thankfully, the money appeared back in our account a few days later. We were happy the issue was resolved and continued business as usual.

Fast forward a month or two and the charge appears back in our account. Apparently, the money the bank originally placed back in our account was a "place holder" until they could better look over the situation. Well, they weren't able to claim it as fraud and couldn't get a refund from the store where the purchase was made. So, that left us without our expected reward. And what was even worse was that we had it and then they took it away! Whether or not that was a fault on their end or our end for not noticing it immediately, we have made sure to not let it happen again. The cake was definitely a lie.

Before we move on, let me clear up what I mean when I say reward. It doesn't have to be a trophy, gift, or money, even though it could be in some cases. It can be anything good or beneficial that comes out of what we are chasing. For instance, when chasing God, a reward might be peace or wisdom, and when chasing your family, it might be having a family that worships together or something as simple as keeping your spouse happy.

As we chase things in life, the reward is what keeps us going and gives us the drive and desire to keep chasing. I'm sure there have been plenty of things in your life that you were chasing that never produced a reward and so you gave up. No worries, I have too. It's our natural instinct to quit something that's not working. God designed us this way for a reason. If we never grasp that and keep chasing-quitting and chasing-quitting, we will live a miserable life.

Thankfully, God has given us an incredible chase that produces the most perfect reward: Himself. When we understand that and, most importantly, act on it, every other thing we chase in life becomes easier, because we are filled with the perfect reward that is more than enough to extinguish any exhaustion and free every frustration.

If you're like me, you read that last paragraph and thought, yes! That makes sense! But I'll be the first to tell you that it's not as easy as it sounds. If it were, there would be no need for me to write this book, and we would all have healthy, growing relationships with God. Luckily, we aren't on this journey alone, and God has given us His word, His Holy Spirit, and other believers to help us along the way.

Why is the reward so important? The actual reward itself isn't necessarily the important part. Yes, in certain situations, the reward is very important and necessary for a proper chase, but what drives each chase is the sense of progress or accomplishment. When we are rewarded during one of our chases, it motivates and gives us initiative to continue chasing or to start

> If we can become chasers that are excited about chasing, there's no limit to what we can do and accomplish!

chasing something else. If we can become chasers that are excited about chasing, there's no limit to what we can do and accomplish!

My guess is you've probably got things in your life right now, other than God and family, that you are chasing, and you are desperately longing for their reward. I've got good news and bad news. The bad news? In the next chapter, I'm going to tell you to stop chasing those things, or at least drastically pull back to get a better view and cast your vision. I know that may be difficult and you might not think you can. But, trust me. The good news far out ways the bad in that, through this book and your journey to become a better chaser, you will be better suited to chase those things while living a less exhausting and frustrating life.

chapter one

CHALLENGE

At the end of each chapter, there will be scripture to read and a chapter challenge with practical steps on implementing the principles from the chapter. Don't skip over the scripture, challenges, or workbook. It all works together and is essential in walking through this book to become a better chaser.

Read Ecclesiates Chapters 3-5 and reflect on it as you do the chapter challenge and workbook assignments.

If you haven't yet, turn to the Chasing Workbook on page 169 and make a list of what you have been chasing and why you have been chasing it. Don't be too quick to answer but answer honestly. Think about where you spend all of your time. Ask God to reveal those things to you, especially those that you may be blind to or unaware of.

chapter two

STOP CHASING

This chapter is going to be difficult for a lot of you, including myself. We are, for the most part, chasing the things we are chasing because we think we have good reasons to be doing so. But, because of that, in order to stop chasing one of them, we have to convince ourselves that stopping that chase is the best option and a wise decision.

Let's be clear. When I say stop, in some instances, yes, it may mean stop. But in other instances, it may simply mean that you focus less time and energy on one of your chases. Obviously, there are things in your life that you have to chase: a job, two jobs, paying rent, paying a house payment, feeding your family, etc.

My goal is not to ruin your life or others' because you gave up something that you needed to be chasing. It is simply to get you to reset your focus and become a better chaser.

WHY STOP CHASING?

We somewhat went over this in chapter one, but it's definitely important enough to hit again. Think back to the game of tag. While our first scenario involved you chasing only one person, most of the time the game of tag involves a whole group of people running and tagging. So, let's say there are ten people playing and you are "it" and have to tag someone. That leaves nine people left for you to tag. How do you go about tagging them? Do you sprint after the group and find the slowest person, dodging back and forth trying to at least tag someone? Or, do you pick out one person at a time, chase them down, and then move on to the next?

Some of you may be on the extremes and favor with only one of those schools of thought, but some of you, including myself, sit somewhere in between. I personally lean pretty heavily towards the "pick out one person" side, but if I happen to be running close to someone else or see someone that might be easy to tag while chasing that first person, I'll do it. No shame.

If you've picked up on it already, you can see how similar this is to chasing things in life. Some of us focus on chasing one or a few things at a time and others chase as many as they can see and run after. We run until we catch something and then move on to the next chase, or we run after one and then another and then another, gasping for air as we seek to catch at least something. Wherever you fall on the spectrum, know that there is hope and that you can become an incredible chaser.

So how does this game of tag relate to why we should stop chasing? Well, the obvious reason is, you'll eventually get tired, especially if there are people faster than you that you are chasing and there's no possible way to catch them. And when you don't catch them, you get frustrated. Another good reason to stop chasing is to chase something else, just like in a game of freeze tag. You chase someone until you catch them, move on to chase someone else, and then eventually have to chase that first person again.

In life, we are always chasing different things, and as previously mentioned, some of us chase more than others. Having the knowledge of when and how to stop chasing them is vitally important.   Without knowing that, we end up

> What things on your list have you been chasing too long?

chasing the wrong things for the wrong amounts of time and never give adequate attention to things we should be chasing the most. What things on your list have you been chasing too long?

DISTRACTIONS

Now the fun part! Not really, but we all love distractions. Don't deny it. You know you love taking your mind off the struggles of life and playing your favorite game, watching that dumb romantic comedy over and over, or mindlessly scrolling through social media. In fact, let's start with social media!

Social media is great, right?! Really! I think it is a wonderful thing and can be used to accomplish a lot, work or non-work related. However, it is abused more than it is used. For time and knowledge's sake, I'll use Facebook as an example, because that was my drug. Relate these next ideas and principles to whatever social media outlets you use.

As you read in chapter one, I was constantly on Facebook. It fed my constant need for something to do and took up so much of my time. The first or second day after I had deleted the app off of my phone, I experienced an eye-opening moment that forever changed how I view extra time and fighting distractions.

My wife and I were sitting on our couch one evening, and she was on her laptop working on homework. We had just finished watching one of our favorite shows, Good Mythical Morning (if you haven't seen it, it's an amazing, ten to fifteen-minute YouTube show that you need to check out), and I pulled out my phone to…check Facebook. I went to tap where the app had been on my phone, and it wasn't there. So, you know what I did? I got up and cleaned the kitchen and dining room! Crazy right?! I would have never considered doing that in that moment if I had Facebook on my phone. I would have sat there scrolling until my wife finished her homework. Don't get me wrong. Sitting with your spouse while you both do different things is great. But, I had the opportunity to do something productive and helpful for our home, and little things like that can be huge in personal growth and in growing your marriage.

It was then that I realized how much time I was wasting on Facebook. And please don't misunderstand me. I love Facebook and still use it, just not on my phone currently. Facebook has been a great tool for my businesses, keeping in touch with friends, planning events, and staying plugged in with my church, and I plan on continuing to use it and even possibly downloading the app back on my phone when I feel it won't be such a distraction. Throughout the day, when I'm on my computer, I'll update my pages and check my notifications. This has allowed my down time to be devoted to more important things, such as reading scripture, planning the next date night with my wife, or simply unplugging from social media and resting my brain and eyes.

> The problem occurs when we mindlessly revert to staring at these apps and scrolling.

I know it would be hard to implement the no phone app principle with apps such as Instagram and Snapchat, since they are phone based, but you can still be intentional about how you use them. The problem occurs when we mindlessly revert to staring at these apps and scrolling. My challenge to you would not be to delete all your apps but to have a purpose when using them.

"For everything there is a season, and a time for every matter under heaven."

- Ecclesiastes 3:1

> *Look carefully then how you*
> *walk, not as unwise but as*
> *wise, making the best use of the time,*
> *because the days are evil. Therefore,*
> *do not be foolish, but understand*
> *what the will of the Lord is.*
>
> - Ephesians 5:15-17

While these verses aren't speaking directly to social media or distractions, it's made very clear throughout scripture that time is extremely important, and we should put forth ample effort in deciding how we spend it.

You may be wandering, though, what purpose we can place on using Snapchat, Instagram, or any other social app. It's not rocket science, and there's no need to make it any more complicated than it has to be. They are built primarily for social connecting and entertainment, and there's nothing wrong with using them for those purposes. But, when we know their purposes, we have to look at our life and how much time we have each day to determine a healthy amount of time to spend on them.

The "purpose" comes into play more so in purposefully SPENDING time instead of mindlessly WASTING time.

There are many ways you can accomplish this but here are a few that have worked for me. You can set a time or location when you are going to use certain apps and stick to it. For instance, I deleted the Facebook app off of my phone which caused me to spend most of my time on Facebook on a computer. Or, you can simply turn off their notifications, so you aren't constantly bombarded with every like, comment, or share. Instead of letting your apps control when you look at them, you have to take control. It's a hard thing to do, but I promise you will feel freer and have more time and energy to

> The "purpose" comes into play more so in purpose-fully SPENDING time instead of mindlessly WASTING time.

chase things that are far more important if you do it.

Beyond social media, there are many things in life that can be distracting: any type of game or gaming system, TV, family issues, new exciting chases, relationships, etc. There are countless things in life that can distract us from what we should be chasing and want to be chasing the most, even if those distractions aren't inherently bad. A very common form of this is known as escapism. This would be our tendency to look for distractions to remove ourselves from reality, or escape reality. Depending on your personality or circumstances in life, escapism may affect you in different ways or not affect you at all. Either way, we have to be aware of where our focus is directed and do our best to be intentional with how we spend our time.

The goal here isn't to get rid of all distractions. That would be impossible, and if you set out to do that, you'd be spending more time running from distractions than chasing your chases. The goal is to minimize distractions. And, in order to do this well, you have to be able to recognize them. If you really spent time on making your first list of what you were chasing and you were brutally honest with yourself, a lot of your distractions should be on that list. In the next section, you'll be prioritizing your list, so try to identify what your distractions are and make sure they are at the bottom of your list. To identify them, ask yourself these questions. Is this chase consuming too much of my time or energy? Is this chase important to God, my family, or me? Is it glorifying God and making me a better chaser? Is this chase necessary?

WHEN DO I STOP CHASING?

Another question we must continuously be able to answer well is, "When do I stop chasing?" How are we supposed to know when to stop chasing one thing in order to chase another? This can be answered fairly easily, but it can be a beast to actually execute well and consistently.

Prioritize. I know that sounds cliché and you were probably hoping for a very deep, philosophical answer, but it really boils down to having a clear vision of what is important to you and what you want to chase.

Refer back to your list from chapter one. If you took the time and were really honest with yourself about everything you are chasing, you should have a pretty substantial list. Turn to the Chasing Workbook on page 171, and take a few minutes to make a new list.

This time, list them in order of importance. (If you have thought of any other things you are chasing since you made that list, be sure to add them in now.) I'll help you with numbers one and two.

1. **God**
2. **Family**
3. **Now, finish the rest until all items on your list are prioritized.**

Now that you have what you are chasing in an order you believe to be best prioritized, circle your top three. Let's spend a few minutes making sure they are truly deserving the time and energy they need to be properly chased.

Ask yourself, "Are any of the things I am chasing from number four and below taking time away from my top three?" The obvious answer is yes, and that's okay! Time has to come from somewhere. We will be working on how to give them their proper time without shorting your top three. Let's look back at your top three and see how the importance of their chase will determine when you stop chasing other things.

In order to make sure your top three are being sufficiently chased, you must first know how to sufficiently chase them. It would be almost impossible to give a specific number of hours every day, week, or month we should be chasing each one and would honestly never work over an extended period of time. The time and energy each chase requires is going to

> Over-analyzing a schedule and chase is where many people fail, and as a result, become bad chasers.

fluctuate, depending on different seasons of life you are in.

While time management is incredibly important, over-analyzing a schedule and chase is where many people fail, and as a result, become bad chasers. They believe if each chase is perfectly and consistently scheduled, everything will work out. But when things don't work out like they should, and the proper time and energy aren't spent correctly or wasted, they feel exhausted, become frustrated, and give up.

Now, don't misunderstand me. Scheduling and planning is a must if you want to be a better chaser, but it's not the perfect answer, won't always work, and honestly, won't result in an enjoyable life. I mean, if you were playing tag everyday with the same people and you knew exactly when and where they were going to run, would chasing them be any fun?

So, if we can't rely on a perfect schedule and set hours to chase certain things, how do we become better chasers and know when to stop chasing? The two best answers I have found are flexible planning and freezing a chase.

FLEXIBLE PLANNING

You can probably guess what flexible planning is just by the title, but to be safe, flexible planning is when you have adequately planned for something and, by doing so, have built in the flexibility to adjust the plans or change them completely. Think back to our game of tag. While a majority of the time you won't be given an opportunity to map out your plan of attack before the game begins, you can at least devise a game plan as you begin chasing. Now, if you decide to only chase one person until you tag them, you may dig yourself into a deep, exhausting hole if you fail to catch them. But, if you plan to chase someone until you either catch them or need to refocus and chase someone else, you'll probably have better luck catching someone.

This idea of shifting your focus within your chases translates to chasing things in life as well. Throughout life, you have to be prepared to stop chases, begin them, and learn how to do that effectively. Stubbornness in alternating between chases in life is as unsuccessful as stubbornness in refusing to chase anyone but the person you can't catch in a game of tag.

This concept has become a staple at my church as we strive to create a better, more genuine worship experience on Sunday mornings. Before each Sunday service, there is so much work behind the scenes that goes into preparing it, and if you work or have worked at a church, I'm sure you understand. The sermon or sermon series has to be planned out. A sermon outline is usually created and then prepared. The songs have to be selected ahead of time and shared with the music team or choir. The music team or choir has to rehearse the music. Volunteers must be scheduled and prepped for their position. I could go on and on about the preparation it takes to pull off a single Sunday morning service. But for us, we don't prepare so we can execute it exactly as we have planned. We prepare so we can be ready for God to move, shift our focus, and develop the service into what He has planned.

You've probably heard the saying "Failing to prepare is preparing to fail." While that can definitely be the case, I tend to look at it more with this attitude as I lead our church in worship: "Passionately preparing is preparing to be passionate." And when this is done well, whether we stay on schedule and follow the line-up for our service or not, we trust that God's plan for our service far surpasses anything we could ever design.

Passionately preparing is preparing to be passionate.

Our chasing has to reflect passionate preparation. We have to know what we are chasing and when we are chasing it, but when God temporarily shifts our eyes to focus on and chase something else, we can't strain our necks trying to keep our focus on what we were previously chasing. We have to learn how to transition our chases with ease, not anxiety or frustration. And when that chase is over, it's vitally important to regain our focus and get back on track with the right chase.

A lot of times, God gives us a warning on an upcoming change in one of our chases, and it's up to us to passionately prepare for that change. With my job, I travel to a lot of different conferences and events, and while my wife is a more important chase than my job, there are times when I have to spend days or weeks away from her to attend these events. Most of the time, I have several weeks or months' notice as to when I will be gone. For me to passionately prepare for that temporary shift of my time and energy from my wife to my job, it's important that I spend extra time with her before and after I go. It's when I don't passionately prepare for these times that our marriage suffers and my chasing gets out of rhythm.

> When God temporarily shifts our eyes to focus on and chase something else, we can't strain our necks trying to keep our focus on what we were previously chasing.

Other times, we have to transition our chasing to other things rather quickly. Although it seems like this could cause a lot of problems, if we have already taken the necessary steps to become good chasers and are passionately preparing, it should be no surprise when they pop up. And when these chases are over, we must regain our focus of what we were previously chasing and get back on track as soon as we can.

FREEZING A CHASE

If you think back to our freeze tag example, you'll remember that even though you were chasing someone and then were no longer chasing that person, you eventually began chasing him or her once again. When strategically planned, freezing a chase (temporarily not chasing something) can work miracles for the other things you are chasing.

Say for instance you don't want to give up Facebook or Instagram completely, but you know they are big distractions and take up a lot of your time. Freezing that chase for a short or long amount of time may be best for you. This would be deleting the app off of your phone, simply not getting on it for a set amount of time, or waiting until the top things on your list are being properly chased before reintroducing it.

Before my wife and I got married, we decided to take the two months before our wedding and stay off of social media so we could focus on each other and prepare ourselves for our marriage. This time was so refreshing, and I would recommend it to any couple desiring to grow closer together, before or after the wedding.

If you do decide to freeze a chase, set a goal. Do you want to freeze it for a certain amount of time, say two months like my wife and I did? Or, would you rather freeze it until your priorities are being sufficiently chased? Either way, unless your plan is to eventually stop chasing it, setting a goal insures that you have a set time in which to resume chasing it. Don't be alarmed though when life happens and a chase has to be unfrozen or you decide you need to freeze it for a longer period of time. While these goals are helpful, don't let your initial approach dictate the best route to achieve them. Again, passionately prepare.

STOP CHASING

By now, I hope you've discovered a few of your chases that need to be frozen or stopped completely. There are things in all of our lives that distract us and pull us away from the most important things we should be chasing. It's okay to have other things you are chasing besides your top three. You always will. But when you become a good chaser, all of those things will find their place in your life without distracting from or destroying your prioritized chases.

chapter two

CHALLENGE

Read Ecclesiates Chapters 3-5 and reflect on it as you do the chapter challenge and workbook assignments.

Turn to the Chasing Workbook on page 171, take your new prioritized list, and cross out the things you need to stop chasing completely. Put an asterisk (*) or a star beside the ones you want to freeze and how long you want to freeze them. If you want to get creative, grab a blue highlighter (because blue is cold right?) and highlight the things you want to freeze or make a new list and draw them with a blue pen, pencil or marker. Make sure to have your top three things you want to be chasing circled or in bold. Ask God for guidance and wisdom on what chases you need to freeze or stop and sit back and listen. Let Him reveal to you what things in your life you should be chasing.

For Him to reveal that to you, He may use your Pastor, spouse, or friend. Surround yourself with people who can encourage you and help keep you accountable, something we will discuss in more detail later. Spend time in prayer and in God's word and always remember: He is our first and most important chase.

chapter three

HOW TO STOP CHASING

Now that you've decided what you want to stop chasing or freeze, you may be questioning how you are going to do that effectively. This is one of the first concrete steps you'll be taking in becoming a better chaser, and it is extremely crucial to the entire process. We will be going over several different principles and practical ways to stop or freeze a chase in this chapter, but your particular situation may call for a different approach or strategy. I encourage you to take the principles and concepts I lay out and adapt them to fit your needs and lifestyle.

ACCOUNTABILITY

Before we jump into different strategies of stopping a chase, it's crucial that you understand you cannot do this on your own. Now, don't cop out and say, "I have God to help me." While that is a correct statement, it is imperative that you surround yourself with at least one accountability partner to help you become a better chaser. Maybe you know of a friend, family member, your spouse, or even your pastor that could benefit from becoming a better chaser. If so, invite them on this journey with you as you both read through the book and work together on your chasing.

The reason having an accountably partner is so important, is they will keep you on track and consistently hold you accountable. Yes, God will give you the strength and desire to

> God designed us to work together as the body of Christ.

become a better chaser, but He won't text you every day, keep you accountable, and encourage you.

The bible instructs us to be surrounded with other believers, and God designed us to work together as the body of Christ. Is it possible to become a better chaser on your own? Absolutely. Some of you will refuse accountability or never attempt to find it. I get that. But, hear me out. Accountability works. It makes the journey easier, less lonely, and even gives us a taste of that reward when we are encouraged by our accountability partner for doing well.

Hopefully, you're considering accountability on this journey and have possibly already thought of the person you want to ask. Go ahead. Ask them. Right now. Stop reading. Seriously, stop reading.

If you still haven't stopped reading to text, call, or message your potential accountability partner, maybe you are unsure of how to ask them. Let me help.

"Hey (friends name)! So, I started reading this REALLY AWESOME book about becoming a better chaser in life, you know, like chasing God and other things that are important. The book has recommended that I find an accountability partner to help me stop chasing certain things and possibly read through the book with, and I was wondering if you would want to be my accountability partner. Basically, I would just let you know what I want to stop chasing and/or start chasing, and you can check in with me regularly to make sure I'm doing it. What do you think?"

Okay, so maybe that was a little much. Or maybe it was perfect! Just don't trek this journey alone. Let's move on to different strategies of stopping a chase.

COLD TURKEY

Stopping a chase cold turkey would be giving it up completely and immediately. This is a drastic step, but it is often needed to fix problem areas in your life. Having accountability is especially crucial for this method. This option may not be for everyone and can be tough. However, it's a great starting point if you feel you are chasing something that you know you shouldn't be chasing, especially if it has been wreaking havoc on your life and causing your other top chases to fail.

Often, when we quit something cold turkey, it may be easy the first few hours/days, but then you may begin to miss what you quit. It's at those moments when accountability can either make or break you.

Maybe you have been chasing a toxic dating relationship that you know you need to give up. Relationships can be a huge blessing or a huge burden on our lives and classifying each as a blessing or burden can sometimes be tricky. Here is another reason why it is so important to have accountability in your life.

Ask your accountability partner if you have any toxic relationships in your life. If your accountability partner doesn't know you well enough to answer that adequately, sit down with him/her and tell them about the important relationships in your life. If you, personally, aren't able to tell if a relationship is toxic or not, having an outside perspective should do the trick. Without the intention of being accountability partners, it's not typical that a friend, often even a close friend, will give you very critical feedback of your other close relationships.

Outside of relationships, there may be other things you feel you need to stop chasing cold turkey. Something I do caution; don't stop chasing something cold turkey that will negatively affect or hurt others, especially your family. (This is more pertaining to quitting a job rather than breaking up with a boyfriend/girlfriend. Chasing toxic dating relationships should be quit cold turkey.) No matter what it is that you need to stop chasing, make sure you are aware of what will happen when you stop, and having that accountability partner can give you a great outside perspective of that situation, as well.

There have been several chases I have stopped cold turkey throughout my life including everything from relationships to social media. One particular cold turkey stop, though, has really played a huge role in part of the tag line of this book, "refocusing our vision on God and family." That stop was the particular way I was pursuing my career with the music studio and label. I was spending so much time chasing leads and doing follow ups that rarely ended in a "reward" that I neglected time with God and my wife. Once I realized that, I completely stopped advertising for the studio and chasing down potential new clients. And you know what happened? More clients started approaching me. It was the craziest thing. I think God often times doesn't give us the things we want until we want Him more than those things. And when we want Him more than those things, those things become less of a priority, and we see how much of a distraction they were to begin with. God knew I needed studio work to bring in money for the company, and when I focused on Him instead of the work, the work became easier.

Now, I'm not saying stop wanting what you want to get what you want. That's not how it works. But, when we focus on God and seek after His will instead of our own, what we want begins to align with what He has, and our chases become more focused and intentional and the distractions seem to disappear. With all that in mind, can you think of anything you need to stop chasing cold turkey to realign your focus back on God?

WARM TURKEY

Sadly, warm turkey, isn't really a phrase people use, but let's go for it. We will classify this as something that you know you need to stop chasing, but you know stopping cold turkey would be a disaster.

Maybe this is a job that you have that's requiring too much of your time and taking away from chasing your family or God. This is obviously something that you need to pull back on, but if you stopped immediately, you would have no income or stability. If this is your situation, ask yourself these questions. If not, hopefully you can relate.

"Are you actively looking for another job, or just accepting the fact of what you have?" "Is this a temporary job with a particular end date or time frame, or a never-ending spiral into retirement?"

Let's look at the first question. Hopefully, if you're not satisfied with where you are already, you are pursuing something else. If not, maybe this is the push you needed. Maybe you aren't looking for another job because

Is your dream job giving you your dream life?

you love this job. Maybe it's your dream job. But is this dream job giving you your dream life? I'm guessing no, if you aren't happy with what and how you are chasing.

Next question. If your job is a summer job or

something to get you through school, those can be tough and can make chasing other things very difficult. In these situations, or any other situation where you really can't quit chasing something due to your circumstances, I encourage you to pull out your list of things you are chasing and evaluate.

> # When we can't change one chase, we can change another.

There are going to be things in life we have to chase, like it or not, that may cause a disruption in what we really want or need to chase. In situations like this, we have to be very strategic with what we chase. When we can't change one chase, we can change another.

Look at the bottom of your prioritized list. There may be one or several things you are chasing that would be easy to stop chasing or freeze, such as your distractions. Stopping these chases cold turkey will quickly free up some time and energy to put towards the chases at the top of your list or those you have no choice in chasing. It's important to tackle those first and then look at the chases you need to quit warm turkey.

The important thing with stopping a chase warm turkey is to never give up. It may take weeks, months or years to stop that chase, but never quit. By taking the necessary steps to free up your time with the chases that are easy to quit and focusing on what matters, God and your family, the warm turkey chases will get easier to stop and will happen sooner than you think.

HOT TURKEY

We all knew it had to come to this, but fear not! This one actually has a turkey reference! Imagine with me. It's late November and you are with your best friends and any family you can stand to be around (I'm trying to create a happy environment for you, not a yapping family meal). The timer for the oven goes off for the fresh turkey you've been cooking, and you run into the kitchen. You open the oven, and the aroma of a perfectly cooked turkey envelopes all of your senses. (I'm sure some of you are sick already if you don't eat meat or hate turkey. Just visualize your favorite food, and we'll still be friends.)

You pull the…favorite food…out of the oven, walk it over to the table and set it down right in the middle. The room erupts with applause as everyone is so excited to devour the…favorite food. You take your seat, pile a portion even too big for your eyes onto your plate, and take the first bite. It's amazing! It's perfect! It's the best you've ever had and will ever have. Pure magic.

You continue to eat and have flamboyant conversations with your friends and family that spark joyous memories and boisterous laughter. What an evening! You finish your fifth plate and lean forward to heap more of that favorite food onto your plate, but…it's all gone. Did you not make enough?! Did your best friends shovel it down like they always do?! Your anger kindles as you sink back into your seat and realize that it had to come to an end at some point. The turkey was perfect, and you would eat plenty more if you could, but dinner is over and it's time for dessert or to start planning the next meal.

There will be things in life, good things, GREAT things, that will end. Ever heard the saying "all good things come to an end"? Well, that's not true. But, a lot of them will. Some are by choice, others by necessity. The point is, we have to be prepared for how we will respond when the great things we are chasing end.

> We have to be prepared for how we will respond when the great things we are chasing end.

There are two ways to respond: You can sink back in your chair, dwell on that anger, and let it drive a series of possible bad decisions, or you can kindle the anger and start preparing for the next chase.

A great example of this happened when I got married. Before I got married and during my engagement, I was chasing a full-time career as a touring musician, and I loved it. I played music that I loved with people that I loved. It was by far one of the greatest experiences in my life. Getting married, though, I knew that traveling full-time wasn't going to be an option for me and my wife. It was then that I had to make the choice to stop chasing that career, find another one, start chasing it, and more importantly, start chasing my wife and family.

> We should always be prepared to stop all big chases in our lives hot turkey.

Most of the time, these "hot turkey stops" will be when you stop a major chase in your life. Sometimes they will be extremely exciting and easy. Other times they will be frustrating and very difficult. We have to decide long before a hot turkey stop that when it happens, we will respond correctly, no matter the circumstances or how it makes us feel. We should always be prepared to stop all big chases in our lives, except God and family, hot turkey. There's usually no way of knowing when they are going to happen, and even when there is, it can sometimes be hard to accept, or it may not truly settle in or hit us until it's too late.

No matter what chase stops or how it stops, you have to be prepared to respond correctly. Identifying the chases in your life is a huge part of that. As you adapt what you are chasing, update your list and always know how to respond when you stop a chase, or a chase stops on its own.

chapter three

CHALLENGE

Read Ecclesiates Chapters 6-8 and reflect on it as you do the chapter challenge and workbook assignments.

Take the time to go through your big chases and prepare for what would be the next chase if they were to stop or you had to give them up. It's never too early to start planning, and you'll be glad you did.

Don't forget to find your accountability partner and go over what chases you need to stop and how you plan on stopping them. If you are still unsure of who that could be, ask God to give you wisdom for choosing someone. Seek His counsel in prayer and by reading scripture on how to prepare for stopping your chases.

Also, turn to the Chasing Workbook on page 173, and answer a few questions pertaining to this chapter.

chapter four

CHASING GOD

There were so many emotions, thoughts, and questions of my own when I sat down to write this chapter. I'll be completely honest with you; I don't feel adequate in telling you how to chase God. Moreover, I feel as if I have some of the right answers and do's and don'ts, but I'm no master at implementing them into my own life. There may be some of you who haven't fully bought into anything I'm saying yet, and after the beginning of this chapter, you may disregard it all and quit reading. But first, let me make my case.

I am a nobody. I am so far from being able to hold a sophisticated, theological conversation. I can only recite a few scriptures from memory. I often have to fan through the entire bible to find an unfamiliar book. I don't pray or read scripture often enough. I don't pray or read scripture with my wife often enough. On Saturday nights I often dread leading worship on Sunday mornings. I often ignore important outreaches inside and outside of the church because I'm tired and lazy. I am a sinner. I am a nobody.

If you had to write a paragraph like I did above, what would yours say? Would it look similar? Would it look a lot better? Would it look a lot worse?

My point is this: It doesn't take a perfect theologian who has the bible memorized and who spends every moment praying, reading scripture, or serving at an outreach to know

> There's nothing harder than trying to get your brain to do something your heart doesn't understand.

that he needs help. Chasing God should be his priority. I may not know it all or be fervent in my walk, but I do know this: I need God, and I want to chase Him with everything in me. Do you?

I could spend the next few paragraphs or pages telling you that praying and reading scripture is how you chase God, but I've heard that so many times, and guess what? It hasn't helped. Before we can get to the "what we do" stage, we must figure out "why we do what we do". There's nothing harder than trying to get your brain to do something your heart doesn't understand.

WHY WE DO WHAT WE DO

We've spent the last three chapters mainly talking about principles and concepts and how they relate to our chases. I want you to take some time now to really dig into scripture and see what it has to say about what we are chasing in life.

Who better to look at than a man depicted in the bible as chasing after God's own heart: David. Throughout scripture, we can see several different things David was chasing such as, God's will, freedom for his people, and leading his children. While all these are great, David wasn't a perfect man and chased things apart from God, such as sexual sin. Nonetheless, David is a great example of how and why to chase God.

Take some time and dig into David's story. Below are several passages illustrating the things David was chasing. Feel free to read more than what I lay out to get an even better understanding of David's life and what and why he was chasing.

- **1 Samuel 17:4-11, 24-49**
- **2 Samuel 5**
- **1 Kings 2:1-4**

1 SAMUEL 17:4-11, 24-49

This is an incredible story of David chasing after what and who he believed in. He wasn't going to let anyone stand up to his God. He knew the power his God had and trusted that He would provide.

And David said, "The Lord
who delivered me from the paw of the

lion and from the paw of the bear will deliver me from the hand of this Philistine."...

> \- 1 Samuel 17:37

Do we know the power of our God and trust Him? I think, sometimes, we forget or diminish the incredible and unmatched power of our God. Thinking about His strength and power alone should drive a desire in us to chase Him.

> We have to create a vision of God that is bigger than our vision of self.

When we "put God in a box" and diminish our view of his omnipotence and authority, we only position ourselves to fall short of worshiping Him like we should. We have to create a vision of God that is bigger than our vision of self. By doing this, we see our desperate need for Him and how big and powerful He was, is, and will always be.

2 SAMUEL 5

In this chapter, we see David become king and get right down to business in defeating his enemies. My favorite part about this chapter is David's full reliance on God and need to seek His wisdom with crucial decisions. Twice, David "inquires" of the Lord.

> *And David inquired of the Lord, "Shall I go up against the Philistines? Will you give them into my hand?" And the Lord said to David, "Go up, for I will certainly give the Philistines into your hand."*
>
> - 2 Samuel 5:19

> *And the Philistines came up yet again and spread out in the Valley of Rephaim. And when David inquired of the Lord, he said, "You shall not go up; go around to their rear and come against them opposite the balsam trees.*
>
> - 2 Samuel 5:22-23

I often find myself searching facts or numbers when trying to make a crucial decision in my life, when I should be searching my heart and scripture to seek wisdom from God ("inquire of the Lord"). One great example of this happened shortly after I started writing this book, and I didn't even realize at the time that's what was happening.

While my wife, Charity, and I were searching for our first home to purchase, we were really clueless. Now, that's not necessarily a bad thing; it just made it more interesting and fun! We both truly had a sense that it was the right time to purchase a house and knew that we were following what God had planned for us. So, as we began our search, we looked through every house online we could find, looked at all the pictures, and read all the info. When we were ready to start visiting a view of them, we set up a meeting with a realtor, who was a good friend of ours. Upon our first visit, he showed us several houses he thought we might like and even emailed us the info on them and several more. Moreover, there was one house he spoke very highly of, but it didn't seem very appealing to us.

Fast forward a week or so, we had picked out six houses from all that he had sent us that we wanted to visit. So, one hot Saturday we set out to view them all. After looking at all of them and honestly being really uneasy about each one, the realtor asked if we would want to see the one he had spoken so highly of, and out of respect and honestly, desperation, we said yes. The moment we stepped in the front door of this house, we knew it was the one. It was perfect and everything we were looking for. How could we have come any closer to missing out on it?! God had clearly placed our friend and his recommendation in front of us only to have it shoved to the side.

While God wants us to seek after Him when making big, and little, decisions in our lives, He doesn't want us to drop Him after we've made the decision. He wants us to continue to walk

> Sometimes, I believe we put more trust in the resources than the One who gave them to us.

> Our imperfections don't affect His perfect direction.

with Him and seek His guidance. For some odd reason, my wife and I trusted God to tell us when to buy a house but trusted the internet on which one to get. Now, don't misunderstand me. Using all the resources God has given us, I believe, is vital in finding His direction in our lives. However, sometimes I believe we put more trust in the resources than the One who gave them to us.

Something that we have got to understand and believe is that God doesn't mess up. His plan is perfect. His people are not, but we are a part of His plan, which is. Our imperfections don't affect His perfect direction.

1 KINGS 2:1-4

Because it's short and such an incredible depiction of how to lead your children, here it is again.

When David's time to die
drew near, he commanded Solomon
his son, saying, "I am about to go the
way of all the earth. Be strong, and
show yourself a man, and keep the
charge of the Lord your God, walking
in his ways and keeping his statutes,
his commandments, his rules, and his
testimonies, as it is written in the Law
of Moses, that you may prosper in all
that you do and wherever you turn,
that the Lord may establish his word
that he spoke concerning me, saying,
'If your sons pay close attention to
their way, to walk before me in
faithfulness with all their heart and
with all their soul, you shall not lack a
man on the throne of Israel.'

- 1 Kings 2:1-4

I absolutely love the beginning of David's charge to his son, and I feel like it can be summed up as this: Chase God. David knew and had experienced what it was like to chase after God and wanted his son to do the same. Even though David never caught God in His chase, which I'm certain he didn't expect to, he chased after God as if his life depended on it. This is an incredible picture of what the top two things we are chasing should be: God and Family. David got it. Of course, he messed up many times, but he was always brought back to the realization that chasing God was most important, and family second.

> When we are grounded in our faith, though trials will come, we will never lose the focus of our primary chase.

When we are grounded in our faith, though trials will come, we will never lose the focus of our primary chase.

Although David is a great example of chasing God and gives us some amazing reasons as to why, he is not THE REASON why. Let's look at a very familiar

passage of scripture, that I believe, if we fully understood
and grasped, should bring us to tears every time we read
it.

> *And you were dead in the*
> *trespasses and sins in which you once*
> *walked, following the course of this*
> *world, following the prince of the*
> *power of the air, the spirit that is now*
> *at work in the sons of disobedience—*
> *among whom we all once lived in the*
> *passions of our flesh, carrying out the*
> *desires of the body and the mind, and*
> *were by nature children of wrath, like*
> *the rest of mankind. But God, being*
> *rich in mercy, because of the great*
> *love with which he loved us, even*
> *when we were dead in our trespasses,*
> *made us alive together with Christ—*
> *by grace you have been saved— and*
> *raised us up with him and seated us*
> *with him in the heavenly places in*
> *Christ Jesus, so that in the coming*

ages   he   might   show   the immeasurable riches of his grace in kindness toward us in Christ Jesus. For by grace you have been saved through faith. And this is not your own doing; it is the gift of God, not a result of works, so that no one may boast. For we are his workmanship, created in Christ Jesus for good works,   which   God   prepared beforehand, that we should walk in them.

- Ephesians 2:1-10

God doesn't need us. We were filthy rags with no hope or help. But, He wants us. He wants us to chase after Him, because He knows without a shadow of a doubt we will find fullness, peace, grace, mercy, forgiveness, and love when we do. He wants us to chase after Him, so we not only come to know Him more, but become more like Him in the process.

Don't get caught up asking yourself, "Why should I chase God?". Instead, ask yourself, "Why does

God need chasing?" This may be too grammatical for some of you and may not even make sense. But, I like it, and it is a good example. God never designed us to be the subject, the main point, or the purpose. He is the subject, the main point, and the purpose. His desires outweigh our decisions. His purpose outweighs our plans. In keeping God the center, or the subject, we are

> His desires outweigh our decisions. His purpose outweighs our plans. In keeping God the center, or the subject, we are forced to rely on what God is doing and wants rather than what we are doing and want.

forced to rely on what God is doing and wants rather than what we are doing and want.

WHAT WE DO

Now that we have a better understanding of the why, let's talk about the what. Before we jump into these next sections, take a minute to read Romans 12 and take note of what it says about communicating with God, reading scripture, and being part of a biblical community.

COMMUNICATING

Be constant in prayer.

\- Romans 12:12b

Praying. I feel like the term "praying" has certain connotations that can lead people to keep it confined to certain standards or settings, so let's use "communicating".

This was an area of my life that I became very

aware of and took advantage of at an early age. The summer before my freshman year of high school, I was diagnosed with Ulcerative Colitis. It is an inflammatory bowel disease that results in ulcers and inflammation in the colon. One of the major symptoms of this disease is diarrhea, and not just diarrhea, but very immediate, with no warning, diarrhea.

If you have this disease or know someone who does, you'll know that being near a bathroom at all times is vitally important. This can make traveling or being in an unfamiliar setting difficult and overwhelming. When I was diagnosed with this disease, I soon became aware that I spent a lot of time talking with God about my bathroom visits, whether that was asking for a few extra minutes or praising him for making it.

You may have a situation in your life that you spend a lot of time talking to God about. That's great! I think it's wonderful when we have to rely on God for things in our life. However, it can't stop there. If the only time we talk to God is when we are in desperate need of something, we aren't fully communicating with Him.

Communication with someone is back and forth, good and bad, fun and sad, and everything in-between. Some people say that "God knows everything, so why should I talk to Him about it". My pastor made a great

> Prayer isn't for the benefit of God; it's for the benefit of man.

point in his sermon recently and said, "Prayer doesn't change God's mind, it changes our heart." Prayer isn't for the benefit of God; it's for the benefit of man.

If you haven't prayed much in your life, give it a shot. Think of it as communicating. Take time to listen to how God moves in your heart and directs your thoughts. Get on your knees and share with Him the incredible things that are happening in your life as well as the bad. Fall before His throne and seek forgiveness and ask to become more like Him.

Getting on your knees and closing your eyes can be great, represents true submission to Him, and really allows your mind to focus, but you don't always have to do that. Try praying out loud or in your heart with your eyes open while you are driving or working. Think about how you communicate with your best friend or someone you like spending time with and treat your communication with God the same way.

One of the ministry team leaders at my church taught me this really cool method of praying. It's nothing new or fancy, and you may have heard of it. It's called ACTS. Adoration (praising God for who He is), Confession (acknowledging your sins and laying them before His throne), Thanksgiving (celebrating how God is moving in your life and others) and Supplication (praying for your needs and the needs of others). While it sounds simple, it has helped me a lot in forming communication with God, and it's super easy to remember!

READING

> *Do not be conformed to this world but be transformed by the renewal of your mind.*
>
> - Romans 12:2a

Reading scripture isn't difficult. Being committed and consistent at reading scripture can be very difficult. This is one of the hardest things for me to do and keep doing. I know that reading scripture is vitally important to my walk with God, and yet, it falls to the wayside too often. Why?

I believe reading scripture can be so difficult because of how we view it. Do you view reading scripture as something that is simply good to do, or do you view it as something that is essential to your walk with God? I think a lot of times I fall into the first one, especially being involved in church and small group where scripture is read regularly. While digging into scripture during those times is important, it's even more important that we do it on our own.

I'm sure you've heard that walking with God

should be a relationship and reading scripture should be treated as such. Think about an important relationship in your life. For me, it is my relationship with my wife. If I only participated in that relationship when we were hanging out with a group of people, I would never get to know my wife intimately and our relationship would never grow. If we only read scripture when we are surrounded with others in the body, we aren't going to have that intimate relationship with God that He so desires to have with us and that our soul's so long to have with Him.

Do you view reading scripture as something that is simply good to do or do you view it as something that is essential to your walk with God?

(This principle applies to communicating with God as well).

We know that we should be reading scripture, and we've probably known it way before we started on this chasing journey together. So, what's going to make this time different than all of the other failed attempts to be diligent at reading God's word? Is it a specially designed reading plan that continually grasps your attention or lays out the scriptures in a way that's never been done before? Is it setting a reminder in your phone that pops up every day? Is it a cool app that reads scripture to you and then shows you a relevant video about how scripture is practical in today's society?

Let me be frank with you and myself. None of those things will ever make you a diligent scripture reader. Don't get me wrong, they can help and be an incredible catalyst, but they won't keep you reading scripture. The only thing that will keep you reading scripture is you.

Think back to that important relationship you have. Is that relationship so great because you watched a YouTube video telling you how to have a good relationship or because you set a reminder every day to text that person? No! That relationship is great because of your desire for it. You saw that the relationship had potential and you pursued it.

A great relationship takes effort. Having and using tools can help speed up the process and make it easier and more accessible, but without YOU, the tools are useless. Being diligent at reading scripture doesn't come from having the right tools; it comes from someone who knows how and wants to use them.

> Being diligent at reading scripture doesn't come from having the right tools; it comes from someone who knows how and wants to use them.

Do you see reading scripture as an integral part of your growing relationship with Jesus? If not, you'll never be diligent at reading scripture. If you do, act like it. Pursue that relationship. Desire to know God on an intimate level and long to become more like Jesus. By all means, download the cool apps and set reminders. But, remember, those will never make you a diligent scripture reader. It's up to you.

COMMUNITY

For as in one body we have many members, and the members do not all have the same function, so we, though many, are one body in Christ, and individually members one of another.

- Romans 12:4-5

Biblical community is one of the most neglected aspects of Christian living. It's almost as if people take the idea of Christ's body being broken, which is used during communion to remember His death and sacrifice, and act it out in their walk with other believers. The body of Christ, the church, is not meant to be broken!

> *And let us consider how to stir up one another to love and good works, not neglecting to meet together, as is the habit of some, but encouraging one another, and all the more as you see the Day drawing near.*

- Hebrews 10:24-25

The importance of biblical community is unmeasurable and necessary for a proper chase of God. How can we stir one another up or encourage one another if we do not meet together? How can the body function properly if all the members aren't present and fulfilling their position? Bottom line…it's not possible.

The excuses for not being part of a church body are endless. If you're not currently involved in a church, let me guess why not. You were burnt by a church years ago and have no desire to go back. You can't find a good church. You don't like the pastors at the churches you've visited. You don't like the music at the churches you've visited. You work on Sundays or during service times. You don't feel welcome at your local church. There isn't a church in your area. You don't know anyone that goes to that church. You get the picture. And whether or not I named yours, any excuse won't keep you from standing before the Father some day and it shouldn't keep you from being a part of His church.

> Surround yourself with other believers, constantly and consistently.

All of that may sound a little harsh, but it's the truth. If you don't get anything else from this chapter, or even this book, get this: Surround yourself with other believers, constantly and consistently. Who you are in community with will depict many if not all of the chases in your life. If you're currently, or were in the past, surrounded by a bad community, hopefully you can see the bad chases that come out of it.

Maybe you do go to a church, but that's all you do. You don't get involved and you don't interact and fellowship with the other believers. If that was how it was supposed to work, there would be no need to gather, and we would all just listen to a sermon and sing some songs on our own. It's very clear in scripture that physically getting together as believers is vitally important. The only excuse that might prohibit that would be a physical illness where you could not attend a service. But still, if you are involved in a community of believers who care about your well-being as a Christ follower, they would visit and bring the community to you.

There are so many benefits to being part of the body of Christ and fulfilling your role as a believer that listing them here would be a book in-and-of-itself. So, just do it. Get involved and get plugged in. There are great churches out there. Sometimes it takes a little digging or driving, but you'll find one. And if you have come to the ends of your resources and do not have a church, email us and we will point you in the right direction. It may even be in God's will for you to start and plant a church in your area. But you'll never know until you seek out being the fully functioning body of Christ that reaches people across the nations with the great news of the gospel.

chapter four

CHALLENGE

Read Ecclesiates Chapters 9-10 and reflect on it as you do the chapter challenge and workbook assignments.

If you're like me, you still want a plan. You still struggle where to turn to when you pick up the bible. So, knowing myself, I can't end this chapter without a plan, and trust me, it's going to be difficult for me as well. As I write this, I struggle to read scripture and setting out a plan, hopefully, will help you and me both.

Whether you are a brand-new Christian, or you've been a Christian for seventy years, there's no better place to start than in the gospels. And if you're like me, you may have read through the gospels several times.

That's okay! You can never over read scripture!

So, let's start in the book of John. My challenge to you and myself would be to read a chapter a day. Even though you're currently reading through Ecclesiastes throughout this book, it will be good to get in the habit of reading something you will continue with once you finish this book. You don't have to read twenty chapters from three different books every day to become diligent at reading scripture. You just have to become consistent. If you want to read more than one chapter of John today, feel free. But don't assume you'll read that much every day. You are excited today and really want to jump in, I know, but life will happen tomorrow or next week and you'll get busy and forget. That's okay. Just start small and stay consistent. Let's jump in! Set down this book and read John 1. No worries, I'm doing it, as well.

Great! If you haven't been consistent in reading scripture, welcome to the beginning of it! It starts on day one. But, don't let it end on day one! Before moving on to chapter five, turn to the Chasing Workbook on page 175 and answer the questions about chasing God.

chapter five

CHASING FAMILY

If I'm being honest, this is the chapter I have been most excited about writing. The previous chapter, unfortunately, was very difficult to write. I know how much I struggle with chasing God, and finding the words to encourage you and myself was tough. Hopefully, you were encouraged and have begun to passionately pursue your relationship with God.

Before we start, here is my disclaimer. My wife and I, currently, do not have any children; therefore, I don't feel adequate in telling all of you parents out there how to chase your children, figuratively or literally. Hopefully, I'll gain that knowledge soon! Moreover, I will be focusing on chasing my wife. Like before, I hope these principles will transcend chasing a wife and help you chase your spouse, girlfriend/boyfriend, parents and possibly your children.

Now, if you are in a dating relationship or are engaged, please be cautious as you read this chapter. I will do my best to encourage you as well, but remember, I am pursuing my wife, which should be treated, in many ways, differently than a dating relationship. Nevertheless, I will do my best not to leave you all out.

Let me begin by saying, I love my wife. I have loved her from the moment I met her. Just ask my best friend, Koltin. While I don't remember this, mainly because I have a terrible memory, he will tell you that after my first date with Charity, I came home and said, "Raise your hand if you're in love!" And then I preceded to raise my hand. Yes, I know. That is completely cheesy, but isn't true love cheesy?

Charity and I have been married two years and twenty-five days, the day that I am typing this. It has absolutely flown by! Now, I know there are some of you out there who have been married much longer and you laugh at me saying two years have flown by. I hear you, and I'm looking forward to many more years!

Before I get into how we should be chasing our family, let me start with how terrible of a job I was doing.

Because I was chasing my career the majority of the first two years of our marriage, I let our marriage almost fall apart. We were both unhappy and rarely voiced it, and when we did, it turned into a yelling match. Then, we would have to back track from all the mean things we would say, or more so, I would say. I wanted the perfect marriage. And by perfect, I don't mean what I saw on TV. I mean what I saw around us from our friends and family. In either instance, neither are good to project onto your own marriage, but still, I wasn't happy with how ours was progressing.

> You can't fix your marriage by chasing your marriage.

There are so many things I've blamed my unhappiness in our marriage on, from her not being understanding of my feelings to me working too much and not spending enough time with her. What took me so long to understand was that I couldn't fix my marriage by chasing my wife. Let me rephrase that. You can't fix your marriage by chasing your marriage. If you picked up this book and started reading at this chapter, you'd have it completely wrong and backwards, and that's what I was doing.

I thought if I could spend enough time with her, plan out our date nights, and do everything I could to make her happy, our marriage would succeed, and I would be happy. That didn't work, won't work, and will never work. Focusing on your marriage to make your marriage work will only offer a temporary fix. Healing and growth in

Healing and growth in your marriage only happens when you focus on God to make your marriage work.

your marriage only happens when you focus on God to make your marriage work.

Even though I knew, from the beginning, focusing on God was the only way my marriage was going to work, it took two years of temporary fixes, countless fights, and finally a very beneficial meeting with us and two of our pastors for it to knock me in the face. I think sometimes we know the right answers so well that we try to find different solutions that look like the right answers on the outside but require less work on the inside.

Marriage is hard, and it takes work. Misdirected work, basically terrible chasing, will only lead to frustration and exhaustion, like we've mentioned many times before. That's where me and my wife were; we were tired and unhappy. Thankfully, we have people in our lives who will sit us down, ask the hard questions, and challenge us to direct our work in the right direction. That's where we are right now, focusing on God to make our marriage work and putting in the effort to see it succeed.

Now, once you have your effort placed in the right direction and you are chasing God in order to make your marriage, or any relationship work, it's time to look at chasing that relationship well.

CATCHING UP

If you were like me in the fact that you weren't properly chasing your spouse or family, you've got a lot of catching up to do. This is by far the hardest part of chasing your family. By now, you may have extinguished any trust from that individual. He/she may be secretly unhappy just as my wife and I were or many other consequences from a failed or faulty chase.

The best and hardest thing to do in this situation is to sit down with the other person and tell them you have failed at chasing them properly and you want to change that. This meeting may evoke lots of frustrations and tears, but it's necessary to conduct a proper chase. Be honest with that person. Tell them why you haven't been chasing them well. Tell them about what you've been reading and encourage them with what you've learned about being a good chaser.

Here are some questions you've got to be able to answer before you start properly chasing others.

1. **Why are you chasing them?**
2. **Where are they going?**
3. **How are you going to chase them?**
4. **When are you going to chase them?**

Answering some of those may be tough, but it will help you in the long run to know the answers. Let me answer them as they pertain to my wife, and hopefully that will help you answer them as well.

WHY AM I CHASING MY WIFE?

I am chasing my wife because she is my wife. I love her more than anything, and I want our marriage to be successful. As my wife, she deserves my attention and to be chased, and I am called to lead her. Through sickness and in health and 'til death do us part, I'll constantly chase and pursue her, ever growing in our marriage and all the while falling more and more in love with every part of her being.

WHERE IS SHE GOING?

This can be a tough question if you don't intimately know the person you are chasing. This question pertains to what they are chasing. Something I have figured out that will come in handy in any chase: If you don't know where someone is going, you can't adequately chase them. Now that doesn't mean they won't make a few quick turns or change direction, but you've got to know a general direction, or you'll never be able to chase them well. Think back to our game of tag. This would be like being "it" and having a blind fold on. You know that there are people running around and that you should be chasing them, but you are completely lost and are running in the dark.

Back to my wife and what she is chasing. She is pursuing God, furthering her education, chasing me, chasing our future family, etc. When I know these things, I can better lead her and encourage her, two vital things in chasing your spouse, especially for a husband chasing his wife. I know what her goals are, and that helps me understand how she feels about certain situations and decisions.

HOW AM I GOING TO CHASE HER?

I am going to chase my wife by pursuing our joint and separate relationships with God. I'm going to pray with her, read scripture with her, go to church and small group with her, and encourage her to pray and read on her own. I'm going to plan date nights, spend time with her, and show her that I love her in the ways that she needs. I'm going to keep her in the forefront of my mind when scheduling and planning things and make sure her needs and wants are considered in every decision. I could go on and on, but you get the picture.

WHEN AM I GOING TO CHASE HER?

I'm going to chase her daily. I'm going to chase her when she needs to be chased. I'm going to chase her even when I don't feel like chasing her. I'm going to chase her even if she stops chasing me.

Hopefully, you've been able to think of some answers to those questions pertaining to the people you want to chase. Again, it takes more than knowing the right answers. It takes effort. Turn to the Chasing Workbook on page 177, and jot down those answers. If you need more space than what's provided in this book, remember, the Chasing Workbook is available online where you can print out however many you need.

IT TAKES EFFORT

These next few sections will be focused on chasing your spouse, more particularly your wife. If you are unmarried, you may not be in the future. Spouses, I encourage you to get your significant other to read along with you, if they are not already. Wives, if your husband won't read along with you, I hate that, but I encourage you to read, and put these principles into practice in your marriage as best you can. Sadly, some men won't chase their wives effectively or at all. If that's the case, wife, you can chase your husband and be an incredible example of what a good chaser looks like.

> Pursuing an intimate relationship effectively is difficult.

Chasing my wife is very difficult. It's not because we've had a tough and challenging first few years together or because I had a lot of catching up to do. She is hard to chase simply because she is my wife. Pursuing an intimate relationship effectively is difficult with anyone. Think back to your relationship with God; it's difficult.

I was always told that marriage was hard, and I believed it. I never thought I would have to put in so much effort though. A quick example. Throughout elementary and high school, I knew exactly how much effort I had to put in to get good grades and be successful, and that's what I did. I worked hard and studied to achieve what I did, and because my focus was on that, I was able to graduate high school as one of the valedictorians.

I tell you all that, not to brag, but to relate it to effort in a marriage. I know some of you didn't care about school or didn't do well, and I know there's a lot of you that did much better than me. That's not the point. My story doesn't end here.

> We have to stop treating our marriages like dating relationships and put in the effort to make them successful.

When I went to college, I put forth the exact same effort I did in high school. With that amount of effort, did I become valedictorian? Absolutely not. I did well, but in order for me to achieve the same success in college as in high school, it required more effort.

Now, relate high school and college to dating and

marriage. See the similarities? High school prepared me for college and took a decent amount of effort. When I got to college, it required more effort to be as successful. In marriage, do you want to just get by and trudge your way through, or do you want it to be successful and to aim for the best? We have to stop treating our marriages like dating relationships and put in the effort to make them successful.

When my wife and I got married, I continued as if nothing had changed. I still pursued my passions and my career and didn't focus on her and giving her the attention she needed. Two years of that can cause a lot of bottled up unhappiness from both parties, trust me.

Thankfully, our story doesn't end there, and yours doesn't have to either. There is hope for an unhappy marriage. But, know this: God didn't design marriage to make us happy or to be fun or rewarding. He designed it to bring Himself glory, to give us an example of his relationship and love for His church, and provide us a way to fulfill our sexual temptations and desires.

When we understand God's design for marriage, we are able to chase our spouse with the right purpose. Instead of trying to make ourselves happy, we will start chasing them to glorify God, and as a result, we will become happy and see the rewards of a fruitful marriage. Like we discussed in chapter one, the reward is an essential part of chasing. If we pursue God and chase our relationships like we should, we will begin to see the rewards, and those rewards will pour into and feed the other chases in our lives.

So, now that we have a full understanding of why we should adequately chase our spouse with the expectancy that it will be difficult, let's dive into what that looks like.

> God didn't design marriage to make us happy or to be fun or rewarding. He designed it to bring Himself glory.

HOW TO CHASE YOUR WIFE

Like I said, this is a very difficult task, not impossible, but very difficult. It takes time, planning, energy and most of all patience. Be encouraged with this, though. Ninety-nine percent of women out there want to be chased. At least there's that right? And wives, if your husband won't chase you, chase him.

There are several things that I have found to be essential in chasing my wife. I'm sure there are plenty more that will work great in your marriage and some I'm sure I'm forgetting that work great in my marriage. But for this section, let's focus on these four.

1. **Lead her in devotion.**
2. **Plan date nights.**
3. **Listen and respond, or don't.**
4. **Make her feel bad. (I'll explain later.)**

LEAD HER IN DEVOTION.

For me, and probably most of you, this has been the

hardest of the four. I think it is the hardest because it is one of the hardest things to do ourselves, and if we aren't doing it alone, we can't expect to do it with our wives. Let's assume you've started praying and reading on your own. Now what? How do you initiate a prayer or read scripture with your wife? It's not easy, I'll tell you that.

I was really encouraged when a pastor told me that praying with his wife is one of the hardest, most awkward things he has to do. He said it was so difficult to pray with our wives because we know them intimately. He said he had no problem praying with strangers or on stage on Sunday mornings, but praying with his wife was challenging. So know, you're not the only one who struggles with praying with your wife.

So, how do we do it? That pastor said he counts to three and then just does it! While that may sound silly, it works! Is what you are doing working? I've found that for my wife and I, it's best to pray at night before she goes to work (she works a late shift.) My pastors also encouraged me to pray for my wife during the morning. This helps with several things. Knowing that I'm praying for her, my wife is encouraged and knows that I care for her. It also helps me grow deeper in love with my wife and directs my thoughts to her needs and wants rather than mine.

Reading scripture can be tough as well and something I still struggle with in leading my wife. We've gone through seasons of reading and doing devotions and then never reading outside of church and small group. I would encourage you to try different things until you find something that sticks. Schedule a time everyday where you open the bible together. Pick a book, read it separately, and then discuss it when you are together. Choose a Christian devotion book and read it together or separate. Watch something together, such as sermons or bible studies online. But remember, it requires YOUR effort, not just the tools.

There are so many great ways to dig into God's word with your wife that we should never not be pursuing one of them. The goal is to pick something and stick with it. It will be tough and awkward, but so rewarding in your marriage and relationship with God. In the first chapter, I mentioned that you can chase more than one thing at a time. Here it is. Leading your wife in prayer and reading scripture accomplishes two things. You are chasing your wife by leading her, but you are also chasing God by leading her in things that focus both of your attentions on Him.

PLAN DATE NIGHTS.

This is something I love doing, but definitely don't do enough. Think back to when you were dating your wife. Think about your first date. Was it elaborately planned out or a date that just naturally occurred? Either way, I bet you can think of a really cool date you planned out for you and her, and maybe that was when you proposed.

Why did you plan the date you are thinking of? Was it to simply impress her and make her want to marry you? Maybe, but let's be honest. For the most part, it was because you really liked her, wanted to get to know her better, and have fun in the process. Are those things still true in your marriage? Do you like your wife? Do you want to get to know her better? Do you want to have fun with her? Your answers should always be resounding yeses to those questions!

So why don't we adequately date our wives once we get married? The obvious reason is that we've gotten what we want, so why keep trying? The goal of dating is to find a girl to marry, and most of us stop there; however, marriage isn't the finish line. It's simply a checkpoint on our particular journey to glorify God and become more like Christ.

When we fail our spouses and disobey God, we don't start back at dating, or at least we shouldn't if we can help it; we start back at the checkpoint, our

> The goal of dating is to find a girl to marry, and most of us stop there; however, marriage isn't the finish line.

marriage. And throughout our marriage, we should constantly be creating new checkpoints, fervently advancing on our journey, learning more, uncovering the curvy roads and how to handle them, and seeking the true finish line, becoming like Christ.

One of the best ways to chase after your wife and those things listed above is incessantly pursuing her, aka, dating her. When is the last time you planned a date night? I'm not talking about a night you two just spent together. I'm talking about a planned, all out exquisite night, that probably cost some money and maybe required a few inside connections of other friends.

To answer that question myself, it's been awhile. Sure, we hang out at the house and watch TV or movies, but that's not what I'm getting at. Although, often times, that's the best we can do. However, it doesn't mean we shouldn't try harder. We need to pursue our wives as if we are still dating them, hoping they will fall more in love with us as we fall more in love with them.

I'll go ahead and roll out a chapter challenge here. Take your wife out on a nice, romantic date. You don't have to spend a thousand dollars but spend something if you can. If you're struggling financially, sell this book and use that money, cancel your TV or music streaming services for a month, stop drinking so much coffee, sell your old gaming console that you don't play anymore but tell yourself you're going to play at some point so you keep it, ask your pastor (if you tell your pastor you've decided to really start dating your wife and that you don't have any money to take her on a nice date, he better help you out, just saying), work a few extra hours or shifts at work, build something out of wood or sticks laying around your house and sell it to somebody. Do you need more? You get my point. You can find a way to give your wife a nice night out.

Yes, yes, yes. I understand. You can have a great date night out with your wife and not spend a dime, and I promise, you'll have plenty of those. But right now, you haven't been chasing your wife well, and she needs to know that you desire her (something we will talk about shortly) and see that you'll do whatever it takes to chase her and treat her like royalty. Man-up and do it.

As I'm sure you've guessed, I'm talking to myself as well, seeing as I just wrote that it's been awhile since I took my wife out on a date night. So, if you felt like I was yelling at you, I was yelling at myself and you just happened to be here. Thanks for tuning in. Seriously, though, we can all do better at chasing our wives and dating them like we should.

Just for fun, and to help me brainstorm as well, here are some not so normal date night suggestions, some expensive, some cheap, and some free.

DATE NIGHT IDEAS

-   Minor league baseball game (major if you can afford it).

-   Any other sporting game, professional or local (high school games can be fun even if you're out of high school or never went to that high school).

-   Day at an amusement park, zoo, aquarium, or anywhere else you can walk around, talk, and do things.

-   Painting (we have a cool pottery shop nearby where you pick out a piece of pottery and paint it).

-   Progressive dinner. Pick your favorite place for soup, favorite place for salad, favorite place for entrée, favorite place for dessert, and then go to all of them in order.

-   Play a sport: tennis, golf, basketball, racquetball, disc golf, etc.

-   Take a tour of a local business (some cool local businesses that I know that give tours: glass factories, ice cream/milk plants, etc.).

-   Go to your favorite grocery store and buy everything you need for a picnic.

-   Go on a picnic.

I hope that at least gives you a few ideas or helps you come up with some other unique ones that work for you in your town. Now, like I said, you don't always have to spend money on date night. You can stay in and watch a movie or go walk around the park.

Don't miss this, though. No matter what you do, plan it and make it special. Call it a "date night". Give it meaning and purpose. Some of you and your wives may like spontaneity, and that's totally fine! Live it up! But for the rest of us, and even you spontaneiters every now and then, try to plan out your date night. Planning it out and being prepared shows your wife that you have been thinking about her and care about her. If she likes to plan, let her plan some too. There's nothing wrong with that, and it can be super fun for you and for her.

Craft your date nights to fit your relationship. All relationships are different and if you chase your wife properly, you will begin to learn how to date her effectively so you both are happy with the results. And remember, chasing your wife takes patience.

LISTEN AND RESPOND, OR DON'T.

Sometimes, when our wives tell us things, they want us to respond. Sometimes, they don't want us to respond. While that sounds easy (I mean come on, there are only two options), I couldn't tell you how many times I've picked the wrong option. And unfortunately, most of us guys make the mistake of just focusing on the listening part when we get married, and for some of us, even that takes a while to figure out.

I've found that in order to keep my wife happy and show that I care about her and support her, I have to respond after listening to her and respond correctly. The tricky part is, there's no one-size-fits-all way to respond. Each situation requires a different response, and I promise you, your wife has expectations of how you should respond after you have listened. And I'll be the first to tell you that most of the time, she isn't going to tell you how you should respond before the whole experience begins.

Do not fear, though. There are a few key ways to respond that I'll lay out. It's up to you, though, to learn when to use each one.

First response. Don't. Sometimes, we just need to listen, and I don't know about you, but that's hard for me. I always want to respond to what my wife says. For example, if my wife had a bad day at work, my first instinct is to tell her how I think it could have been better if situations were handled differently. RUN FROM ANY FORM OF THAT. Sometimes you just need to listen and let her vent.

Second response. Respond opposite of how she is acting as she is talking. For this response and the next, I'm going to use the same example as above. If my wife comes home from a bad day at work and is extremely frustrated, sometimes she needs to be encouraged, loved, held, you get the picture. She is mad and frustrated, so I act happy and calm. In this situation, the emotions balance each other out, she feels comforted, and hopefully starts to come out of the bad mood.

Third response. Respond exactly how she is acting; empathize with her. Same situation, bad day at work, and she is frustrated. Sometimes, she wants me to be frustrated with her (not at her, but with her) and understand and feel her pain/anger. In these moments, I have to agree with what she's saying and stay on her side. Even if I believe she is wrong in her views, now is not the time to voice that.

Over time, you'll learn when to use which response. The biggest thing you need to get is knowing your response is vitally important. While listening is great, your wife needs you most in the moments after the listening, not just during.

Some of you, especially wives, may be thinking, well that's not fair. My husband is just playing me or acting a certain way to get his way. No. It's about us husbands understanding our wives and being everything they need in those moments.

MAKE HER FEEL BAD.

If you were getting excited about this because you wanted to make your wife feel bad, shame on you. It was simply an act of trickery to peak your interest if perhaps you were getting bored reading this book, which I know is comical. It simply means: Make her feel **B**eautiful, **A**ppreciated, and **D**esired.

This point is a bit difficult for me to lay out. All of our wives are different, and they feel beautiful, appreciated, and desired in different ways. This one is last because it will become easier to do as you perfect the first three. If you lead your wife, date her, and listen, making her feel B.A.D. will come naturally.

Furthermore, I know you understand why it's important that she feels those things, so I won't bore you with those details. But, until you get darn good at reading/praying with her, dating her, and listening/responding, keep B.A.D. in mind in everything you do. Make that a priority in your marriage. You can thank me later.

> If you both have similar slots of off time, use that to your advantage and spend it together.

Here are some practical ways you can make your wife feel B.A.D. First, include her in decisions. Even if she isn't present or can't give her input, think about how she would respond. For me, this has played a huge part in my work scheduling. With her working odd hours at her job, it's very important that I do the best I can to schedule my work hours accordingly and make myself available when she's available. A lot of you, I'm sure, can't schedule your own work hours. That's totally fine. Just be intentional about your time away from work. If you both have similar slots of off time, use that to your advantage and spend it together.

Another way to make sure she feels B.A.D. and possibly the most important, is to find out HOW you can make her feel B.A.D. Most of the time, if your wife isn't feeling those things, it's not because you aren't trying; it's because you are trying the wrong things.

When we get married, our natural

> We have to show our spouses that we love them in the ways that they need to be shown.

instinct is to reciprocate love the way we want to be loved. While in some cases that may work, it's not always the right answer. We have to show our spouses that we love them in the ways that they need to be shown. If you haven't yet, check out the five love languages[3] test. It will give you a great place to start in how to show love to your significant other.

FINAL THOUGHTS

Marriage is difficult. Family is difficult. From the moment sin entered creation in the garden of Eden, the relationship with God and man, and man and man (woman) has been disrupted. Despite its difficulties, God had a purpose and still has a purpose.

> *Husbands, love your wives, as Christ loved the church and gave himself up for her, that he might sanctify her, having cleansed her by the washing of water with the word, so that he might present the church to himself in splendor, without spot or*

wrinkle or any such thing, that she might be holy and without blemish.

- Ephesians 5:25-27

To me, that's an incredible purpose! What a parallel! God is using something that we can experience or witness to symbolize Christ's relationship with the church! Let's look a little deeper into those verses.

Husbands, love your wives, as Christ loved the church and gave himself up for her.

- Ephesians 5:25

Do you get that, husbands? Christ "gave himself up" for her. Does that sound easy? Does that seem effortless? No way. If your marriage is tough right now and you don't feel like chasing your wife, stop feeling and start working. You shouldn't have to feel good or be happy to work on your marriage. Marriage takes effort and will be difficult. But, its reward is beyond explanation and surpasses any argument, frustration, fight, or hurt feeling that will ever arise.

I really hope you feel encouraged, challenged, and like you've got a lot of work to do in your marriage and your family. We should never stop chasing our spouses or family. Christ never stopped chasing

If your marriage is tough right now and you don't feel like chasing your wife, stop feeling and start working.

his people, the church, and even sacrificed His life for her. We have to understand the bigger picture. It's not about our happiness; it's about His glory. It's not about our feelings; it's about His glory. And when we get that and treat our chasing that way, we find that happiness and feel the fullness of His reward and blessing.

chapter five

CHALLENGE

Read Ecclesiates Chapters 11-12 and reflect on it as you do the chapter challenge and workbook assignments.

I have already given you men one challenge. Take your wife out on a nice date. Secondly, I want you couples to pray and read scripture together. If your spouse won't do it, pray that God will work on his/her heart. Stop right now, pray, and read whatever chapter of John you are at. If you've already read John today, great! Read it again! Just kidding. You don't have to do that.

Thirdly, husband, learn how to listen and respond to your wife. Try different responses. A lot of the times, you'll find you have time to jump around them all until one starts working really well. Wife, if you're reading this with your husband, know he is trying; it may take some time, but he will get there.

Singles, no worries. I haven't forgotten about you. Be prepared for marriage, even if you don't plan on getting married. Get everything in place with chasing God so chasing your spouse or any other relationship will come easier. If you plan on getting married, pray for your future spouse and that God will begin preparing him/her for you as well.

Finally, turn to the Chasing Workbook on page 179, and answer the questions about chasing family. I know that's a lot of homework, but these are things we should all already be doing. Like I said before, we have to get busy.

chapter six

chapter six

CHASING LIFE

Once you've focused your vision on chasing God and your family, you can use any of that extra time and energy to chase anything you want! Okay, not anything, but a lot of things. This could include your career, a hobby, or any other thing that you enjoy that isn't terrible for you or your family.

There is something I want to point out, though, before we dig too much into chasing life. Even though our priorities are hopefully in order now, it doesn't mean that we shouldn't be cautious. Things that we chase in life can quickly become idols and take necessary time away from God and family. So please, be careful.

Here's the catch with chasing things in life: They become easier to chase when we are chasing God and our family properly. Why? Think about it. If we aren't properly chasing God and our families, we are going to spend a lot of time fixing problems, expelling unnecessary amounts energy and time, and focusing on trying to continuously get our "life" in order. I'm completely blown away that we even have time to chase anything else when those things aren't in order. But, the good news is that when they are in order, it offers time and freedom to chase other things in a healthy way.

CHASING YOUR CAREER

Chasing your career can be a very exciting and yet, daunting task. Obviously, if it's a career and not a job you are chasing, you are passionate about it and chasing it should be fun (at least some of the time). Being good at what we do, succeeding, and moving up the "corporate ladder" is something we all desire at least a little bit. Nobody wants to fail.

There are some issues that come along with chasing your career, and if not monitored properly, can cause a lot of problems. The biggest issue is expecting a reward from it and then not getting it at all or not getting it soon enough. This reward could be a promotion, pay raise, getting your own business off the ground, etc. The truth of the matter is this: There is no way for us to know when or what's going to happen, and the moment that we think we've got it all figured out, we will discover it's also the moment it all starts to fall apart. Only God knows when a reward is coming from our career (if any); therefore, we have to put our hope in the One who knows, not the one who guesses.

Another issue that comes with chasing your career is the commitment of time and energy. If you want to be successful, you have to put in the effort to make it happen. This can pose a problem. There will be times when you feel it's one hundred percent necessary to

> We have to put our hope in the One who knows, not the one who guesses.

> There's no good excuse for a failed chase of God or your family, not even your career.

be chasing your career, but yet you fail to chase God and your family. How do we combat this conflict? The answer is simple, but the action is hard. You just know.

If you are pursuing God and your family like you should and you are in tune with those chases, you will instinctively know when one of them needs more attention. Though you see and feel that chasing your career is vital and necessary to advancing in it, you will know that pulling away for a bit is worth chasing after God or your family like you should. There's no good excuse for a failed chase of God or your family, not even your career.

A third issue, which may not pertain to you, but is very present in my life, is working from home.

Although working from home can have many benefits, it can also cause a lot of problems if you aren't careful. For me, it caused me to spend way too much time working. Because I work from home and love what I do, I always want to get more stuff done. And if I'm not working, I'm thinking about it. There's not a separation of work and home or work and family. It all blends together, and that can be dangerous.

If you work from home, here are a couple of tips that have helped me. Set a schedule (which we will dive more into in a minute) and share it with your spouse or accountability partner. This will keep you focused and accountable. Next, create a separate work space in your home. For me, that space is my studio. If I'm not working, I try not go into my studio space and focus on spending time with my wife or God. Or, that may be another room or simply a desk. Wherever or whatever it is, give it purpose. These may not sound like groundbreaking ideas, but I promise they make a world of difference when implemented correctly.

So how do we chase our careers affectively? With purpose and planning. Know why you are chasing your career and what the outcome should be. If you know you're going to be gone on a business trip, plan extra time to chase God and your family before and after you go. Chasing a career should be fun, scary, thrilling, nerve-wracking, and whatever else you want to call it. But it should never destroy or chip away at chasing God or family.

You may be wondering how I chase my career affectively. If not, here it is anyway. Relate this how you will, but I know we are all in different scenarios and times in our career. Like I mentioned in a previous chapter, I am heavily involved in music. My passion is growing the label and studio I own and helping young artists.

For me, chasing my career was becoming a problem in my marriage. I was letting it take up too much of my time and energy, and it drastically pulled my focus away from God and my family. In return, those chases began failing. I had to really pull back on how much I was working and thinking about work (which is just as bad for a marriage as working can be).

One of the biggest steps I took was to look at how much time I had each week and decide how much

I should spend working. It may be different for you, and that's fine, but for me, it was forty to fifty hours a week. I usually put in thirty to forty with the church I work for, and then the rest goes into the label and studio. I created a note on my phone that I update every Saturday or Sunday, that lists when I'm working the following week. I total the hours at the bottom and make sure it's less than fifty. Below that, I'll list what I have to do during the work time and also create an off list, which is comprised of things I plan to do when I'm off. To give you an idea, here is what it was for this past week.

TK Work

- Monday 9-5 NH Office – 8
- Tuesday 9-230, 4-9 – 10.5
- Wednesday 1-9 – 8
- Thursday 2-5 NH Office – 3
- Friday 9-5 – 8
- Saturday – Off
- Sunday 8:30-12:30 – 4

Total 41.5

Work

- Edit sermon AV

- Mail CD's

- Edit minute video

- Edit RC video

- Update app and website

- Mix [Artist's] song

- Work on [Client's] website

- Edit church videos

- Edit/Mix [Client's song]

- [Artist] in studio

- [Client's song] tweaks

- [Artist] in studio

Off Time

- Read [Book]

- Clean house

- Finances/pay bills

- Take out trash

- Loan meeting

- Write

While that may seem like a lot, it has been super helpful. It keeps me on task, and I cannot tell you how much of a difference it's made to have scheduled off time. There's a big difference in deciding to stop working for the day or deciding not to do anything for a few hours and actually planning for a day off. It seriously renews your spirit. Try it.

I also share this note with my wife so that she can keep me accountable and know exactly when I'm working. There's nothing worse than her thinking I'm not going to be working one evening and expecting to spend time together only to learn that I have to work. I have to be respectful of her time and feelings. Preparing her for when I'm working and planning it out makes a world of difference.

Though that's a great plan and a cool list, know that it doesn't always work out like I want it to. I'll end up working more here or there or needing some extra time off one day. Still, having a plan and having this laid out, makes those adjustments much easier on my wife and I. Remember, passionately prepare.

I know a lot of you can't create your own schedule or set your hours. That's completely okay. It's still important to have that laid out for you and your spouse (if married) especially if your hours change every week. Knowing your schedule(s), whether work, school, or what have you, is vitally important to be a good chaser.

For those of you stuck in a job you hate or if you are struggling to find your career, know that there is still purpose in God's plan. He has you in that job for a purpose. Instead of complaining and never being happy with it, find your purpose. Is there a co-worker struggling in his marriage or needing someone to share the gospel with him? Maybe you are the only joy your co-workers or bosses see.

Whatever your purpose is, the sooner you find it, the sooner you'll be motivated and find a glimpse of that happiness you so long for. If you are searching for a career or job you love, keep searching and chasing. Make that a chase that falls right under family and really pursue it.

CHASING EVERYTHING ELSE

Quite a heading for one little section, huh? Maybe you still don't believe me, but I promise that once you are chasing God and family like you should, everything else becomes easier. Think of chasing God like one lens in a pair of glasses and chasing family like the other lens. If you've got both lenses in, you can see everything clearly. If you're missing one or both, you'll be tripping all over the place and running into walls. Think back to my cold turkey stop when I changed how I pursued clients for the studio and label. When I gave up that chase, everything seemed to fall right into place. In that instance, it was almost immediate, but often times we won't see results that soon or even see the results that we thought we would see. But, with the right focus and vision for our chases, our priorities fall into place and our plans begin to line up with God's will for our lives.

Vision in life leads you; clear vision in life leads you in the right direction. And when you have clear vision, chasing anything and everything becomes so much easier. But, occasionally, your glasses will get smudged or sometimes broken. But just because your glasses fall off, get smudged, stepped on, or shattered, it doesn't mean you've lost your vision. It means your vision is blurred. And the more you wear those God and family lenses, the easier it will be for you to tell when your vision is getting blurry, because you are so used to seeing clearly.

Becoming a good chaser is all about vision and focus. When you've got God and family in your sights, chasing them becomes easier, and as a result, so does everything else. I feel like I could give you plenty more analogies about chasing, vision, and the like, but I hope by now, you've gotten the point. Before you head to the workbook, let's end with this bit of encouragement for you and myself.

> Vision in life leads you; clear vision in life leads you in the right direction.

BECOMING A GOOD CHASER

God wants us to be good chasers. He designed us to chase after Him and put in our make-up the desire to chase after other things. If we don't accept the fact that we should be good chasers, we will roam this world aimlessly, possibly

> Don't think you'll always be a bad chaser because you've yet to be a good one.

stumbling into a few good chases, but never truly being the kind of chasers God wants us to be. So, if God designed us to be good chasers, do you know what that means? It means, we can be good chasers! There is hope! Praise the Lord!

Don't think you'll always be a bad chaser because you've yet to be a good one. In order to chase, we have to, at some point, be still, not moving and not chasing. We aren't dropped into this world running full force. We've got to gain our focus and vision and then start running. Here's another analogy. Can you tell that I just love them?

Have you ever decided to start exercising or working out and ended up doing way too much on the first day because you were excited? And then, because of that first day, you ended up quitting all together. Been there done that! Most of us are going to want to jump right in and start chasing full force, and that's awesome that we are excited and pumped to become good chasers. But, that may not be the best way to start. For some of you, you may already be decent chasers and you can start running. For the rest of us, chasing things properly may be a new idea or plan for us and we need to start walking, not running.

Pace yourselves. This isn't something that's going to change overnight. It takes time, and it might take a lot of time. Every one of us will become a great chaser in different ways and in different times. Evaluate your life. Look at your prioritized chasing list and be honest with yourself about how much work you've got to do. And be prepared to put in the effort to get the work done.

I am astounded at how much my life, career, and marriage has changed for the better as I have implemented these principles. I am so excited for you and your journey, and I hope you become the best chaser this world has ever seen!

chapter six

CHALLENGE

Read Ecclesiates Chapters 11-12 and reflect on it as you do the chapter challenge and workbook assignments. If you are married, Read Ephesians 5:22-33 as well.

Now, head over to the Chasing Workbook on page 189 and complete the questions about chasing life.

chasing workbook

This workbook is to be used in conjunction with the book as you read it. Throughout the chapters and at the end of each chapter in the Chapter Challenge, you will be directed to turn to this workbook, read scripture, fill out information, and/or answer questions.

By no means is this workbook exhaustive. I encourage you to really dig deep into the principles and questions in this book and uncover even more information about you and what you are chasing than what's laid out in the book.

This workbook is also available online at www.whatarewechasing.com and can be downloaded and printed off if you prefer not to write in the book. My hope is that through answering the tough questions about what and why you are chasing, you'll be able to reveal some truths about yourself and your life. It's only when we have a full understanding of what and why we are chasing that we can make the necessary adjustments to fix any problems.

Take your time when answering these questions and be honest with yourself. Spend time in prayer and really seek how God is wanting to move in your life and make you a better chaser.

chapter one | chasing workbook

CHASING LIST

List the things that you are currently chasing and briefly explain why you are chasing them. Take time to think about them and be honest. Remember, these are things where your time and energy go. Here are some examples you may want to write down: Job, Career, Education, Friends, Family, Kids, God, Social Media, Hobbies, Working Out, etc. Be as specific as possible.

1. _____

2. _____

3. _____

4. _____

5. _____

6. _____

7. _____

8. _____

9. _____

10. _____

11. _____

12. _____

13. _____

14. _____

15. _____

16. _____

17. _____

18. _____

19. _____

20. _____

Feel free to jot down more than on the space available above! There's no shame in being honest with yourself about what you are chasing, and that honesty will make becoming a better chaser much easier.

chapter two | chasing workbook

IMPORTANCE CHASING LIST

Refer back to your original list. Now, list those things in the order of their importance in your life. If you have thought of any other things you are chasing since you made that list, be sure to add them in here. I'll help you with number one and two.

1. <u>God</u>
2. <u>Family</u>
3. _____
4. _____
5. _____
6. _____
7. _____
8. _____
9. _____
10. _____
11. _____

12. _____

13. _____

14. _____

15. _____

16. _____

17. _____

18. _____

19. _____

20. _____

21. _____

22. _____

23. _____

24. _____

25. _____

26. _____

27. _____

28. _____

29. _____

30. _____

chapter three | chasing workbook

HOW TO STOP CHASING

What are the big chases in your life that could change and that you need to be preparing for?

_____

_____

_____

_____

_____

_____

_____

_____

_____

_____

Who is going to be your accountability partner?

_____

_____

What chases do you plan on stopping and how do you plan on stopping them?

_____

_____

_____

_____

_____

_____

_____

_____

_____

_____

_____

_____

_____

_____

_____

_____

_____

_____

_____

chapter four | chasing workbook

CHASING GOD

How often do you currently pray and read scripture?

_____

_____

_____

_____

Why have you found it difficult to be consistent at praying and reading scripture?

_____

_____

_____

_____

_____

_____

_____

_____

_____

_____

Why is it important to you that you pray and read scripture?

_____

_____

_____

_____

_____

_____

_____

_____

_____

_____

When are you going to pray and read scripture?

_____

_____

_____

_____

_____

_____

_____

chapter five | chasing workbook

CHASING

SOMEONE

Who are you chasing?

_____

_____

_____

_____

Why are you chasing that person?

_____

_____

_____

_____

_____

_____

_____

_____

_____

_____

Where is he/she going?

_____

_____

_____

_____

_____

_____

_____

How are you going to chase that person?

_____

_____

_____

_____

_____

_____

_____

_____

When are you going to chase that person?

_____

_____

_____

chapter five | chasing workbook

CHASING FAMILY

For Married Men

What do prayer and reading scripture currently look like in your marriage?

_____

_____

_____

_____

_____

What do you want it to look like?

_____

_____

_____

_____

_____

_____

_____

_____

_____

When are you going pray and read scripture/devotion with your wife?

_____

_____

_____

_____

What are you going to do for your date night with your wife, and when are you going to do it?

_____

_____

_____

_____

_____

_____

How well do you listen? How can you listen and respond better?

_____

_____

_____

_____

_____

What are ways that you can make your wife feel B.A.D.?

_____

_____

_____

_____

_____

_____

_____

_____

_____

_____

_____

_____

_____

_____

_____

_____

_____

_____

_____

_____

_____

chapter five | chasing workbook

CHASING FAMILY

For Married Women

What do prayer and reading scripture currently look like in your marriage?

_____

_____

_____

_____

_____

_____

What do you want it to look like?

_____

_____

_____

_____

_____

_____

_____

How can you help your husband lead you well? If he hasn't been reading with you or does not chase you, how can you chase him?

_____

_____

_____

_____

_____

_____

_____

_____

_____

How can you react better to your husband's response when he is listening to you?

_____

_____

_____

_____

_____

_____

_____

How can you play a significant role in dating your husband, whether or not he is pursuing dating you?

_____

_____

_____

_____

_____

_____

_____

_____

_____

_____

_____

_____

_____

_____

_____

_____

_____

_____

_____

chapter five | chasing workbook

CHASING FAMILY

For Singles

What do you want prayer and reading scripture to look like in your marriage or relationships?

_____

_____

_____

_____

_____

_____

_____

How can you prepare yourself now to make sure that happens?

_____

_____

_____

_____

_____

_____

What areas in your dating life or your relationships in general do you think you can improve on? Listening? Pursuing? Responding? Etc.

_____

_____

_____

_____

_____

_____

_____

_____

_____

_____

_____

_____

_____

_____

_____

_____

_____

_____

_____

_____

_____

chapter six | chasing workbook

CHASING LIFE

Are you chasing a career, or do you feel stuck in a job? Why?

_____

_____

_____

_____

_____

_____

_____

How can you pursue chasing your career or job without it negatively affecting chasing God or your family?

_____

_____

_____

_____

_____

_____

_____

What other things in life do you want to chase (refer back
to your list if you need to) and how and when are you
going to chase them?

_____

_____

_____

_____

_____

_____

_____

_____

_____

_____

_____

_____

_____

_____

_____

_____

_____

_____

_____

_____

_____

notes

1. See www.dictionary.com/browse/chase

2. See Proverbs 10:2-28

3. Moody, and LaCroix Design Co. "Discover Your Love Language." *The 5 Love Languages*®, www.5lovelanguages.com/.

www.ingramcontent.com/pod-product-compliance
Lightning Source LLC
LaVergne TN
LVHW041218080426
835508LV00011B/992